Fatigue - I am enthusiastic a[...]

Heartburn - I w[...] gr[...]
pg
59
e fully. I am safe
I trust the

Onion of The Soul
"Peeling back the layers to uncover the True Self"

Indigestion 49 — process of life

I digest & assimilate all new experiences peacefully & joyously.

Knees/joints
change

I easily flow with change. My life is Divinely guided and I'm always going in the best direction.

Copyright 2018 by A. Annette Hankins

Self-Published

I take in life in perfect balance

Dedication

This book is dedicated to my daughters, Allyson and Allyssa. These two wonderful human beings gave me a true sense of purpose. The love that I feel for them goes far beyond what words could ever express. They have been by my side ever since they came into this world by showing me their support, their love and their care. Thank you Allyson and Allyssa for all that you have been to me. I love you dearly.

My Son-In-law Quincy is the son I never had. He has been a great husband and father to my twin granddaughters. What Son-in-Law would be open and totally receptive to his Mother-in-Law moving in with them on the other side of the world? He has been a Godsend to my daughter Allyson and to my life as well.

My two granddaughters, Kayla and Kamilah have stolen my heart. They look so much like my daughters when they were babies it's like raising my daughters all over again at the same time. I pray they always reach for their greatest self in all that they do.

Lovingly yours,
Momma/G-Ma

Acknowledgements

This book would not have been possible without the inspiration and support from certain people that I was blessed to have in my life. With a grateful heart, I would first like to acknowledge God who is responsible for my very existence. I want to acknowledge my biological and adopted parents and my late ex-husband, Donald. Much gratitude to my daughters, Allyson and Allyssa for their love, support and helping to bring out more of my hidden qualities and strengths. My son in law, Quincy who has been very supportive and encouraging, my sisters, Gloria, Deloris and Barbara, my brother, Galen Story, my cousin/sister girlfriend Brenda Wilson, my Spiritual brothers, Dr. Stanley H. Waldon, Dr. Anthony Ingram, Rev. Frederick Simpson and James Womble, my Spiritual sisters, Judy Womble, Dr. Connie Jackson, Beverly Stephens, Roz Whitney, Linda Clark, Versella James, Rev. Naomi Hughey, Rita Cox, Rev. Eve-Lynn Garnett, Rev. Stephanie Walsh, Rev. Naomi Mitchell, Rev. C. Diane Johnson, Rev. Tonya Lee, Rev. Shaun Gardner, Min. Gwen Whitfield, Jackie Simpson, Diana Lewis, and Marie Hankins. Many thanks to my Hartford Memorial Baptist Church family and The Alice Millar Chapel community and my support team, Mary Kelly, Chaplain Tahera Ahmad, Dr. Timothy Stevens, Dr. Margaret Barr, Marge Bradford, Carolyn and Bill Gifford and Beverly and Omer Reese who were all very helpful during my years as a seminary student while trying to find my direction. I want to thank my cousins Albert Bone, Michael

Bone and Tony Bone and my aunt Willa and Aunt Thelma. I have much gratitude and love for my pastor and father in the ministry, Rev. Dr. Charles G. Adams who was instrumental in helping me recognize my gifts and spiritual leadership. Rev. Dr. Jeremiah A. Wright, Jr. and Rev. Dr. Frederick Haynes were also instrumental in my spiritual development and support and encouragement. I would also like to acknowledge Dr. Sylvia Gray and the late Dr. E. Delbert Gray for their faith in my abilities in writing and challenging me to dig deeper within myself to find the hidden qualities that are uniquely me. Much gratitude goes out to Dr. David L. Snead who was a huge support for me during some very difficult times in high school. He was a great father figure to me who gave me good advice and challenged me when I felt like giving up.

I would also like the thank those who have challenged me and worked my last nerve, took advantage of me, used me and abused me. Because of your treatment towards me, I continued to move forward into the strength that has made me who I am today. Even if I became sidetracked because I was licking my wounds, these negative experiences were lessons that helped me to understand parts of myself that only surfaced when they were stirred up. As Rev. Freddie Haynes said in one of his sermons "the flavor only comes out of the tea bag after it is put in hot water".

Last but not least I want to thank my dog Alaya. She has been a great source of inspiration and support. During my down days, she was there to lick away my tears and show me unconditional love. She was there at the door when I returned home after a hard day, happy to see me and show me love. I would not have been able to write this book without her. During my happy days she made them happier.

Remembering all these awesome beings in my life has given me the ability to begin and continue to peel back the layers that have covered my soul.

Thank you and I love you all

    A. Annette Hankins

Table of Contents

Dedication and Acknowledgements

Table of Contents

Introduction

Chapter 1 Exposing the Pain

Chapter 2 The Layer of Abandonment and Rejection

Chapter 3 The Layer of Trauma & Abuse

Chapter 4 The Layer of Low Self-Esteem

Chapter 5 The Layer of Acceptance

Chapter 6 The Layer of Denial

Chapter 7 The Layer of Anger

Chapter 8 The Layer of Fear

Chapter 9 The Layer of Trust

Chapter 10 The Layer of Forgiveness

Chapter 11 The Layer of Secrets and Lies

Chapter 12 Conclusion

Resources

About The Author

Introduction

Is There Something Wrong?

What's wrong with me? This is a question I'm willing to bet we all have asked ourselves from time to time. When we didn't get the job or promotion we prayed and worked so hard for but it was given to someone else, we ask the question, "What's wrong with me?" When that certain someone did not return the love we have shown to them and they choose someone else, we ask the question "What's Wrong With Me"? When our parents don't show us love and affection and contribute in a positive way to our development as a child we ask the question, "What's Wrong With Me"? When people around us call us names or constantly say negative and demeaning things to us to the point that that way of thinking becomes our beliefs about ourselves, we ask the question, "What's Wrong With Me"? There are so many reasons why people ask this question. My question was usually based on my circumstances. I was always able to find someone or something that was the basis for me needing to ask this question. But during the time of writing this book, I have come to the conclusion that it's not the "someone" or "something" that has caused me to ask this question. It was my perception of who I was within my relationships with others and the part I played in the circumstances.
I began writing this book during a time when I was dealing with different layers of the onion of my soul. As I thought about my

struggles I saw them as layers that covered my soul and prevented me from being the person I'm suppose to be.

Willing to confront the Pain

I feel like the various struggles, fears and issues in my life have covered up my soul and camouflaged my true self. I've been working to identify and peel back these layers so I can evolve into my authentic self.
I'm going to be honest with you. This process is not for everyone. I say that because some people will not be able to face the existence of these layers of their life at this time because this process can and will cause some discomfort and pain. It requires honesty and a lot of inner strength. It can be difficult to look at these parts of our lives and not be effected by them. Some people may want to go through the process but may not be ready at this time. I speak from personal experience on this point. Ten years ago I was not ready to deal with these aspects of my life. The thought of them created too much pain so I once again blocked them out and put a fresh Band-Aid on them and continued living the life that did not represent the true me. But after I decided to go through this healing process, there have been times of fear and apprehension. As I thought about shedding this false persona that I had been living that covered up my soul, this would also release the authentic me who I really did not know. What am I really like and would I like the me who I find? As this transition takes place and I began to shed those old habits that are comfortable and normal to me, what does it

look like on the other side? Will it be like getting to know a stranger? All of these questions plagued my mind. But I had to realize that this was just another layer that I needed to shed. I had to trust that who I was underneath all of those layers of false representation, had to be someone who was real and authentic and represented all the buried dreams and aspirations that I have always had. I had to realize that I already knew the authentic me. I just kept it imprisoned by the bars of falsehood. This process for me has brought out many emotions. I have cried a lot as I recognize the pain that I was holding inside. I also got angry, sad, lonely and agitated. But I knew it was part of the process. The ego is represented in those layers and as I come face to face with them, the ego is strong and will put up a fight.

Finding what works

Many people have tried self-improvement programs, manifesting, meditation, etc. and haven't achieved the results they set out to accomplish. I also felt stuck when these various techniques did not work. But when I began reading and listening to certain meditations that focused on clearing out my negative beliefs which represented the undercurrent of my thinking and belief about myself in my present ego-centered world, I understood why my results were lacking. With these roadblocks or what I choose to call, layers covering up our soul, it is very difficult to reach those goals. Many people have given up feeling that those feel good techniques were not working for them. Instead of giving up on yourself and your lack of significant progress, find a meditation, book or article that helps you find out what those negative blocks are. This book is only the beginning of self-revelation and working toward that goal.

I am not trying to pass myself off as an expert or someone who has had years of experience in this area, but I'm writing as someone who is traveling on this road of inner healing and discovery. I want to share with others the journey that I have taken and will continue to take as someone who is determined to peel away the layers of negative thoughts, feelings and beliefs that have held me back from what and who I am.

Disclaimer

Some people may attempt to peel back the various layers in their life but realize that it is too much to handle at this time. That is ok. I would recommend seeking professional counseling or therapy to help you get the process started. Seeking professional help is not a sign of weakness. It is actually a sign of strength. A counselor or therapist will be able to guide you along at the pace that you need to go. Some can only deal with one layer at a time while others find that several layers are connected and through their recognition and healing they will be able to shed multiple layers at a time.

If you truly want to break free from the false self that you are living and re-discover the you that is buried deep within, I invite you to come on this journey with me.

Why Focus on The Negative?

Some people may wonder why I will focus so much on negative feelings and thoughts. Simply put, that is where the pain resides. If I learned only one thing from studying pastoral care and counseling it is – meet people where they are at that present moment. In other words, acknowledge their present position, acknowledge their pain. This is important because it gives them permission to do the same. I know when I was in pain and I mentioned those feelings to some people, many of the responses were to just get over it, or that I should pay attention to my blessings and not focus on the negative, or it wasn't that bad or just pray about it and give it to God. When people are in pain emotionally, mentally and spiritually, those approaches don't work and can make matters worse. It tells them that it's not good to acknowledge their pain, or their pain is not important. This can lead to more pain and postpone their healing. That's why I'm writing this book to help people know that their pain is valid; their pain is important and should be acknowledged. Everyone has the right to speak their truth. Not what someone else tells them their truth is. As a child I was not allowed to share the truth of my pain and hurts if I did they were dismissed and deemed unimportant. It's an ongoing discovery of my truth is so many aspects but I have begun the journey and so can you.

Out of respect for those who are still living, I will not use the real names of my parents in the description of my past.

Chapter 1

Exposing the Pain

Waiting for the Sunrise

*When will the sun come up and burn this dew off of my heart.
I need the sun,
I crave the sun,
please rise with your promise of a new day, a new me and new feelings other than this pain.
I thought I made it through the night. But this night is the longest night ever, the longest night in the darkest part of the earth.
When will the sun rise so a new day can begin, a new me can emerge out of this dark and painful me.
Nothing grows in the night,
the darkness of the soul is infested with grief and stagnation.*

The Eruption of My Pain

I hate who I am right now. Because I can't stop this pain in my head and my heart over this man who does not give a damn about me. He says he's my friend and he cares about me but it's only in words. He does' nothing to show his care for me or that he's even my friend. I want to hate him so bad but I feel so stupid that I love him. I don't want to love him anymore, I don't want to think about him any more but he stays in my head and my heart like dew on the flower before the sun comes up.

I've been in this darkness before, it looks familiar but I promised myself that I would not enter this darkness ever again but I took a wrong turn, or maybe I took a familiar turn that looked like the right way to go but I ended up back in this all too familiar darkness. Familiar pain, familiar heartbreak, familiar frustration that I'm once again in a place I don't want to be.

Where do I go, I want it all to go away, I want to hit myself in the head and the thoughts go flying out of my ear. Flying out into the space of nothingness where they dissipate into the air and float up into the ozone layer never to be thought of again. Or do I use a knife, to cut out that part of my brain that won't stop thinking of him. Cut it out like cutting a bad part off of a cantaloupe and throwing it into the trash to be buried in a landfill somewhere never to be seen again.

The thought of him, the sound of his name, driving by his office and the memories flood over my mind. Even walking into my apartment causes him to take up residence in my already overwhelmed thoughts. MAKE HIM GO AWAY. I don't want to think about him ever again. But I do. I hate him but I love him. Two totally different thoughts and feelings from different ends of the spectrum are intertwined tying me up in knots.

It makes me so mad when I think about all the wonderful memories we could have. All the places we could have gone, the things we could have seen together. But I'm stuck in "what if" land, we could have, should have, everything was set just perfect for us to be, and do and create wonderful memories.

Sometimes I feel like I just want to die. I ask God why did you create me, if all I was going to have was pain in my heart. You wouldn't let my daddy be my daddy, or even let my father be emotional available. I am a daddy's girl with no daddy. I am a wonderful girlfriend without boyfriend a good wife without a husband. What's wrong with me that they don't want me around, they don't want me, they don't love me? You made me for no one. I give my heart away but they don't want it. My life is a joke to you, I'm tired, I'm tired of the pain, I'm tired of the hurt, I'm tired of being perfect for no one. I can't continue to live like this, no job, no money no man to love me and help me and care about me. What good am I to this world?

Putting it in Perspective

These are the words I wrote one day when the pain was so intense I had to sit down and allow that pain to spill over and emerge from my fingers. I sat at my desk, crying and typing. Typing with my eyes closed and allowing myself to feel the pinned up sadness, loneliness, rejection and anger that had

I need a new normal! without alcohol + nicotine

plagued within me for so long. One thought lead to another revealing a path of familiar choices and disappointments that seemed like an unending freeway of unhappiness. Many of us have traveled along similar paths of life that seems to resemble a rodent on its wheel in a cage that goes around and around and around getting nowhere. We travel on this path so many times it had become our normal way of life. I call it dysfunctional normality. It's not what we actually want or desire but we play a part in attracting the same kind of occurrences because we are attracted to what our normal has been. I decided that I needed a new normal. This old normal was no longer what I wanted in my life. No matter how familiar it was, I was tired of the pain that this "normal" was causing in my life. *so true!*

Where to Begin

My first step was to admit that the original painful occurrence happened. Many times we don't want to or are able to call it what it was. Secondly, I needed to recognize the triggers that caused me to end up in this all too familiar place. Then I needed to determine what I wanted my new "normal" to look like. Finally, I needed to treat myself the way I wanted others to treat me. But what I discovered was, before I could accomplish anything, I needed to learn how to love myself. People think this is a no brainer but actually many people who are honest with themselves do not love themself. The test is something I learned from the great Louise Hay. Her past was more traumatic than mine but she has developed ways to help

☆ important pages

turn her life around and shared this with us, no matter our past. This test is simple but difficult as well. I had to look into my eyes in a mirror and say "I Love You". The first time I tried it, I had to look away because I realized at that moment what I already knew, that I did not love myself. But that was not a surprise to me. I knew for years. I was always made to feel inadequate ever since I was a child. Others rarely told me that they loved me. I was adopted and felt out of place and unwanted. I was provided for materialistically, but my emotional development was underdeveloped. From my conception I was unwanted. When my mother found out she was pregnant with me she talked about aborting me. I was the product of an extramarital affair so to the outside world, I was a mistake. This is how my earthly life began and that feeling of being unwanted continued in my life. So whenever I end up on the bad end of a relationship, all those memories and feeling of rejection and abandonment resurface and the pain grows even stronger.

Daddy Issues

Because I didn't grow up knowing my biological father and my adopted father was emotionally absent, I realized one day during my adulthood that I have serious daddy issues. I truly believe I would have been a daddy's girl. I was a tomboy and wanted to learn how to do everything that a father would teach his daughter. I believe that my choices in the types of men I had relationships with were subconsciously filling my daddy void. I say this because all of the relationships I had were with me at least 10 years older than myself. My husband was 29 years older than me. After this last relationship went bust, I began writing this book and it reminded me of the cycle I was in with the way I chose the men in my life. I realized that I needed to dig deeper into my issues, my layers and begin to heal. I have to work these things out within myself before I think about another relationship with someone else.

Being Honest about My Pain

One of the main lessons I learned in therapy is to be honest with myself and understand what my triggers are. When I am able to recognize the triggers, I am better able to diffuse them or be better able to navigate the situation and myself in the situation.

Most of us spend the greater majority of our lives running from our pain. I know this is true for me. There are certain issues in my life that cause so much pain and discomfort that I choose to force them back into the recesses of my mind. I thought that I could get on with my life and be happier if I did not pay attention to my inner pain.

Within the emotional expression at the beginning of this chapter it contains many of the layers depicted in the following chapters.

Abuse – This comes in many forms, emotional, mental, physical and spiritual.

My abuse occurred mentally, emotionally and spiritually. *self richeousness*

Abandonment and Rejection – These layers occurred in my life from my conception.

Fear – This layer takes the form of holding on to tightly in my relationships. This comes across as being controlling and needy. My fear of losing people in my relationships has caused me to hold on too tightly. This includes boyfriends, husband, daughters, etc.

Anger – This layer is focused on myself and the people who I feel have rejected me. Every time I experience rejection, my anger for the other people as well as my anger towards myself emerges.

Blame – This layer cases the blame myself and those who I feel have hurt me and rejected me, including God.

Denial – I was in denial about putting my past hurts and pain aside and function successfully in a relationship.

Low Self Esteem – This layer deals with my inability to love myself and acknowledge that I have worth and that I matter.

Forgiveness – This layer is represented in the anger that keeps resurfacing towards all who have hurt and rejected me. I haven't forgiven them and

> I haven't forgiven myself for continuing to go down the path of this "normal" behavior.

These layers represent my triggers. Each one is an area I must work on to eliminate in my life. I may not be able to get rid of them permanently but I can diminish their effect on my relationships and myself. Forgiveness is a huge part in helping me with the rest of the layers. I will get into that more in chapter 10.

If you have made it this far in this book, I applaud you. I know I started out this chapter pretty strong. But I wanted to express genuine hurt and pain that not only occurred in my life but also occurs in many people's lives every day. This not only affects women, but men as well. My desire is to help the victims of this pain. I want them to know that they are not alone and it is OK to feel the pain by acknowledging its existence. This will help in the healing process and the ability to let go of that pain. If you have to stop reading this book and put it on the shelf because it has uncovered some areas that are in desperate need of healing, therapy or counseling, please do that. My only concern is that you be healed from those layers of pain in your life so you can live into the person you were created to be.

Chapter 2

Layer of Abandonment and Rejection

Poem

Why did you reject me? The mistake that was made was yours not mine. Why must I pay the price for your mistake? Then you choose to adopt me but deny me love. You make me pay for your anger with her.

This situation that exist is of no fault of mine but I am the pawn sometimes visible sometimes not.

I spent years rejecting me because of you but no more.

My life has meaning and purpose.

I have to learn to love me no matter what you or my past has to say.

From the Womb

My abandonment issues began even before I was born. My mother talked about aborting me when she found out she was pregnant. You see I was the result of an affair she had with her friend's husband. My mother's husband was in jail and she already had 5 children. How could she possibly even consider another mouth to feed in her situation? Her doctor concluded that her pregnancy was too far along for an abortion so she had to figure out another option.

After much discussion her sister told her that she would adopt the baby and raise it as her own. The baby was born and taken to live with her sister. You may wonder why I speak of myself in the third person. I do this because whenever my adopted mother told me the story of my birth circumstances, she always referred to me as "the baby" and never as "you". The cloud of rejection and abandonment followed throughout my developmental years.

We All Need Love

Whenever I talk about my circumstances to some people, some say that I should not focus on the negative but be thankful that I was adopted and provided for. That is true. I am thankful for the roof over my head, the food supplied to me, my clothes and various opportunities provided for me. But people who were shown love and given an emotional connection during those critical years do not understand what it is like to be void of that very important aspect of the developmental process. We are all searching to be accepted and loved for who we are. Material things cannot take the place of that longing.

The Constant Battle

The abandonment and rejection during my life has taken a toll on me. It had become a pattern with people I cared about and loved. The pain of the relationship I vented about as I began the chapter on "Exposing the Pain" has occurred several times in my life. A different face and a different name but the results were the same. I had given my all to these relationships subsequently losing myself in the process. I know that there are many women reading this who can identify with my experiences. We are taught that we are the caregivers; we should take care of those we love. But we are not taught to take care of ourselves. We are not taught to love ourselves.

Starting Fresh

During my years in seminary, I felt like I was starting a new life and tried to put all those old feelings and failed relationships behind me. I was starting new. I was determined not to go down that road again. But then I found myself falling into the same trap I had experienced before only worse. Because I had not taken the time to heal from the layer of abandonment and rejection, it reared its ugly head once again to let me know that it had not gone away. Putting it out of my mind and acting like it didn't exist does not work. It just lays dormant and strikes when you least expect it. My plan was to just enjoy this man's company and have someone to spend time with. I would see him when I wanted and only when I wanted. What I didn't know was that he was a master manipulator and knew how to read my insecurities and me. He knew how to pull my strings. Instead of seeing him when I wanted to, I began to see him when he wanted. When he didn't want to see me, he made sure it didn't happen. There were times when I would ask him about unkind things he either said to me or did and he knew how to turn it around and make me feel like either I was wrong or it was my fault. I then spent much time over analyzing him and me and our situation, because it wasn't really a relationship but a situation. But I had invested so much time and emotions in this situation, I felt like it was a relationship. I had lost myself again. I felt like I was drowning in a sea of negative emotions about myself again. I began kicking myself for allowing this to happen to me once again.

Knocked to my Knees

After feeling rejected and abandoned by this man, accused of being close to a breakdown by a school official who I trusted and considered a friend, and losing my job that I worked so hard proving that I could do, I was knocked to my knees. These were three major rejections within 1 year. But the events that cut even deeper consisted of feeling the distance between me and my oldest daughter and losing my best friend to death all shook me to my core. To say the fight was gone out of me was an understatement. I spent a long period of time just existing from day to day wondering why I was still among the land of the living. The area of my life that once pulled me out of these sad times were my daughters. But I can't count on that any more because my oldest is grown and married and dedicates her life to her husband and God. Part of my brain understands that but not really. I have to stop myself from analyzing what happened to our close relationship. My youngest daughter is now 21 and spending more time with her friends. At times I feel like I don't have anyone any more. I have always had someone in my life that I cared for, but now I only have myself. This should be a good thing, right? I am now free to do what I want and be who I want to be. The problem is I've spend so much time taking other people's needs and considerations that I don't know what I really want or who I am. At times I think I've discovered this allusive me but other times I'm back to square one. It's been very frustrating trying to figure this out.

One morning I went outside to walk my dog and it dawned on me that I've reached a point of feeling that there is no fight left in me. The struggle of finding a job, trying to figure out where I'm going to live have taken precedence over what I want to do. I know they are tied together I just couldn't see it at that time. I have basic survival needs and I don't know where they are coming from. I've read books and listened to meditations of learning how to let go and allow God to lead me into where I'm suppose to go. But nothing happened. Yes patience is part of this but when you've got bill collectors calling it makes it kind of hard to just do nothing. But when the fight is gone and that numbness overtakes my mind, I just feel like walking right into nowhere land.

A Change is Coming

But I know that there is something coming. Part of me can feel it deep down inside. The patience factor is lingering with hope in the fact that it's not time for me to abandon God or myself for that matter. God has not abandoned me even if I felt like He has at times. I now realize that those were the times when I abandoned myself. When I recognize and embrace myself I also recognize and embrace God because I am His creation. Loving God, loving myself and then my neighbor are the basics in survival skills as a human. This is what we are taught in the Bible. It does not mean to love our neighbor before ourselves, as many are lead to believe. The Bible says to love our neighbor as ourselves. This means that love for our self comes after loving God and before we love our neighbor. Because this has been understood in the reverse, many people do not love them selves. I was one of them. We cannot properly or authentically love others if we do not love ourselves first. We have to feel worthy of love before we can show that same love to others. Too many times I based my worthiness of being loved by others. I had to realize that the love I was searching for does not come from outside of me; it has to come from the inside of me, from myself, which is from God.

Acceptance

Underneath this layer of abandonment and rejection is acceptance and the genuine love of God, love for myself and real love for my neighbor. What I had to realize was that the main person who had rejected and abandoned me, was me. It has taken me a long time to figure this out. After all I had to start from ground zero because of the abandonment and rejection from my inception. It's very hard to break a pattern that has followed me from such an early stage in life. I'm not saying that I have completely overcome this, but I am on my journey of recovery. I have a better understanding and know that I cannot just put it in the back of my mind and ignore it any longer. Recognition and knowing the triggers when I see them will keep me on this path of recovery so one day I will shed this layer of the onion of my soul.

Chapter 3

Layer of Trauma & Abuse

Poem

What was done to you is not my fault.
Why do you take it out on me?
I was an innocent child
needing love and acceptance.

What could I have possibly done to be tied to a chair.
The chair was physical, emotional and mental torture.
Tied to your control.
You controlled my mind and my heart.

It's time to free myself.

Reactions to Trauma

Trauma can take many different forms in ones life. A terrible accident can be so traumatic that in order to survive, a person may never want to drive again. This would be their way of coping with the event. A child may stop talking as a way of coping with a traumatic situation. A traumatic event in a child's life does not have to come from a physical event. It can be any unexpected single event or repeated event that makes them feel powerless in preventing it from occurring.

Tied to a Chair

I suffered a traumatic event as a young child. This event was so hurtful that I blocked it out of my mind. My "godmother" was the person who caused this deep trauma. I put it in quotes because this was the title given to her but she was far from why a godmother's role was created. I have never liked my "godmother" even as a baby and was always apprehensive around her. As an adult I realize my inability to forgive her even after trying very hard. One day my Aunt Thelma revealed to me that my mother told her when I was visiting my "godmother" as a young child my "godmother" tied me to a chair. This is how my mother found me when she arrived to pick me up. After hanging up from talking to Aunt Thelma, I cried uncontrollably. That pain that was buried so very deep had emerged. I needed someone to talk to. Someone who I thought cared enough to allow me to express those feelings that had emerged. I called one of my friends who I talk to often and I allow her time and space to talk about her cares and concerns. After she listened to me, her response was, "I wish your aunt had not told you that. You didn't need to hear it." I immediately shut down. Once again my feelings were not being validated. My friend did not see the part that information had in my healing. She could not see that I needed that missing piece of information that played a part in my dislike for my "godmother". It is important to find someone to talk to who will allow you space for your true feeling to emerge. People who criticize and shut you down for expressing those feelings can and will do you more harm.

After my mother passed away, the memories of her verbal and emotional abuse became overflowing in my mind. My mother and "godmother" both enjoyed putting me down and letting me know the many times I did something wrong. Even around my friends, they liked to bring up things I did wrong and laugh about it. I never could understand why my mother would let someone who tied me to a chair remain my godmother. This also plays a part in me forgiving my mother. This kind of treatment also adds to low self-esteem.

Recycled Evil

As I listened to a sermon one day by Bishop Timothy Clark on "Recycled Evil", he talks about how the evil things people do to us can be recycled by God into a positive event in our lives. But we must take those evil things and give them to God by releasing them and forgiving the person. Bishop Clark equated the evil that people do to others as garbage and trash we put out for the sanitation workers to take away. As he talked about how we have to separate different types of trash and put them in recycle bins. The truck takes these items to a plant to be put though a process so they can be used for useful items the same way God can take the evil in our lives and recycle them to be useful situations in our lives. But one thing stood out for me that Bishop Clark didn't talk about. In order for the truck to pick up the recycled items, we must first gather them up and put them out to be picked up. This may seem like a no brainer but if we are so attached to articles, stuff, evil, bad thoughts and other things that do not mean us any good, the recycling process cannot take place. From a trash perspective, when people cannot bring themselves to throw away items that can be recycled but keep their house cluttered with them, hoarding can result from this behavior. If anyone has ever seen the show "Hoarder", you have seen how someone's inability to part with "stuff" can pile up and take over his or her physical existence. Now take that same concept and apply it to our inability to throw out mental & emotional garbage. We can turn into mental and emotional hoarders. Our mind and our heart can stay cluttered with all that evil stuff that can hold us back from living the life that our soul is destined to live. It's time to recycle the evil.

Reclaiming the Music Within

I heard Dr. Wayne Dyer make a statement one day that touched me very deeply. He said "don't die with your music still in you". The reason this statement was so profound to me is because I actually know that there is music shut up deep inside of me. When I was a child I took piano lessons, as did most children. But as I practiced every day I realized that I could eventually play the songs from memory. I also enjoyed playing around with the notes to see the sounds they made. My piano teacher was very strict and very scary to me. If he thought my fingernails were too long, he would take nail clippers and cut my nails so close that my fingers would hurt. As I played the music I rehearsed at home, I found myself not looking at the music because I knew it from memory. One day my teacher realized I was not looking at my music and told me to point to the music that represented where I was playing. I was unable to do that since I wasn't looking at it. He became very angry with me. I heard later from other students that he hates it when people play by heart. Needless to say that every time I went to my piano lessons I was terrified. Because I was so filled with anxiety playing the piano in front of him, I did not play with the same enthusiasm and my lessons suffered. This was reported to my mother and she scolded me in the car on the way home. I still wanted to play music so I started playing the violin in school. I became so good at it that my teacher asked me if I wanted to try the bass. Playing the bass was a lot of fun. My mother noticed that I was excelling with the violin so she decided to sign me up for violin lessons with my piano teacher. Needless to say he took the joy out of playing the violin as well. I continued to play the piano and the violin and was learning to play the organ with a different private teacher but the joy and enthusiasm was gone. My musical heart was lost and eventually I traded in music for

my music?? — dancing suzy my partner. quit nicola

sports. When people ask me if I have ever played an instrument I tell them yes but my teacher scared me out of playing. This is where Dr. Dyer's message hit a homerun with me. I sat down to my daughter's keyboard at home one day and began playing one of the songs I still knew by heart. As I played I felt a deep, extremely deep sensation of music literally welling up inside of me to the point that I began sobbing uncontrollably. I felt so much music inside of me that it felt like it was imprisoned and screaming to come out. That had never, ever happened to me before. It was many years before I even attempted to play again because that feeling was so terrifying. Ten years later as I am reading and studying about consciousness, and gaining a better understanding of who I am, I came across Dr. Dyer saying "don't die with your music still in you". I immediately thought about that day of musical rumblings while sitting at the keyboard. I realized that I had to find a way to satisfy my musical abilities. I knew that I needed to heal from my early childhood musical trauma before I could tackle the music lying dormant within the recesses of my soul. That musical trauma with my first piano teacher is the layer that hides the musical expression of my soul. My music is locked inside me and I'm still working on peeling back that layer which will allow me the freedom once again to sit down at the piano or pick up my violin and play the music of my soul.

Don't Pass on the Trauma

Many of us have been traumatized by others who themselves have experienced trauma in their lives. Recognizing and beginning the process of healing from our trauma can help us on our life's journey as well as sparing others from the fall out of our experience. I say this because un-healed people who have been traumatized can and in many instances do traumatize others because of it. We often hear in the news of people who abuse children have also been abused and traumatized as a child. How many children have been victims of someone else's pain? I am a survivor of another situation by someone who was the victim of a traumatic situation. My adopted mother suffered a traumatic experience that I will talk about later in chapter 10 on "Forgiveness". She came from a generation that did not speak of their bad experiences. They were taught to keep their skeletons in the closet. What happens in the family stays in the family as their motto. They actually believed that if you did not speak of your bad experiences they would go away. This type of thinking is detrimental to the victim and those around them. I have read that in situations like this, the trauma not only grows like a cancer within a person it can also metastasize to those around them. Because my adopted mother denied her traumatic experience thereby not giving herself the ability to heal from it, she acted out that anger and pain onto me. My emotional needs were undeveloped as a child because I feel she projected her pain onto me.

Abuse

Abuse has many ugly faces. When most people think about abuse they focus on the physical or sexual abuse of a person. Not only does this type of abuse cause physical scars, they also create mental and emotional scars that many people do not realize. Because this very important aspect of abuse is not been taken as serious as abuse that occurs on the physical body, it is difficult for healing to occur. Even if the abused person mentally forgets or intentionally puts these very hurtful occurrences in the back recesses of their mind, they remain and can and will wreak havoc on ones life.

Emotional, mental and spiritual abuse can also occur when physical and sexual abuse is absent. I've read that a child who grows up with under-developed emotions is a prime candidate for emotional abuse. A parent or caregiver, who is unequipped or unable to show love or develop an emotional connection with a baby and or child, can produce an underdeveloped emotional child and adult. I feel this adult can go either one of two ways. Either they can become needy by searching for love when and wherever they can find it or they can become hard and emotionless, thereby carrying on that same quality that impacted their life.

This is my understanding from the reading I have done over the years. I started reading on this issue while in my 20s. I needed to know why I felt the way I did. I was the emotionally needy result of parents who were emotionally absent from my life. Not only did I not feel love from my family, I also felt like I had to work to try to gain their love. Something I never felt like I achieved.

Mental Abuse

I suffered mental abuse as a child and as an adult. This can occur when a person constantly hears negative things about them from others. Being yelled at, talked down to, not being supported or valued all play a role in mental abuse. My mother yelled a lot. Especially when I did something wrong. When I did something right, the majority of the time it was ignored. Everyone wants to know that they are accepted. We also want to feel like our thoughts and feelings matter. When the opposite is shown on a regular basis, I feel this is mental abuse and those negative thoughts and feelings about oneself create low self-esteem.

Mental abuse also crippled my ability to deal with conflict. Because of certain dominating people in my family, my conflict resolution skills were underdeveloped. My personality played a role in this as well. I am more of a feeling type of person who cares about other people's feelings. I am compassionate and try hard to be understanding. Because of these traits, I was considered weak. My mother, being the most domineering person in my life, laid the foundation for my reluctance in dealing with conflict. Even when I spoke up for myself or tried to explain my actions, I was ignored and my feelings were not considered. This was the beginning of shutting down for me. I learned early on that I was not being heard or understood during a conflict so I learned how to just listen to what was said by the other person. I felt powerless and usually internalized how everything was my fault. When other people around me realized this, they didn't have to worry about me actually participating in a conflict so I was used, manipulated or ignored. My brother as well as the children at school teased me and I felt powerless to do or say anything about it. Even as an adult, I run from conflict. There were times when I would almost have an anxiety attack just thinking about a possible conflict with someone. I spent a lot of time during my lifetime feeling like I was a weak person because I didn't know how to handle conflict or a heated discussion with someone. If I was forced into a situation, I reacted in an angry way mainly because I hated being involved in it. Afterwards, I would always regret that I let someone push me into that mindset.

    Because of this defensive mechanism from an early age, being silent and not voicing my opinion or feelings has caused people in my life to get frustrated with me for not saying something when they thought I should. One of my sisters, who I grew up calling my cousin, is also strong willed and has a dominating personality. I had to live with her for a while after leaving seminary. She allowed me and my dog Alaya, to move in with her. I was very appreciative but it challenged my ability to take care of myself. Being an independent person and an introvert, I was very sad inside. My sister tried to pressure me into talking about what was going on with me, what was I thinking, what was I feeling? I wasn't ready to talk about it. Being an introvert, I need time to process my thinking and then feel comfortable in vocalizing it without sobbing tears of discontent. When I did feel comfortable in saying something, instead of listening, she began to tell me how I should feel, what I should think and gave her opinion of what she did or would do. All of this just made me go even deeper into my shell of not talking. It was just like living with my mother all over again. When I realized this, I felt even worse. How could I be 54 years old and still be experiencing the same thing again?

Sexual Abuse

I feel that sexual abuse can also occur without the action-taking place. I have two memories that fit into this category. The first one happened when I was about 5 years old. My teenage cousin was over our house and when I came out of the bathroom after taking a bath, he was sitting in my bedroom. Everyone else was downstairs. I stopped at the door. He told me to open my robe. Being 5 years old, I only knew to do what older people told me to do. I opened my robe and he smiled as he looked at my small naked body. Thank God that's as far as it went and he got up and walked out of my room and downstairs. I remember feeling really strange after that but I didn't know why. I never told anyone about it. The second occurrence was when I was about 17 years old. I was the only one home that night. I was talking to my mother on the phone when the doorbell rang. I told my mother to hold on while I answered the door. It was my uncle. He came in and we hugged. But this hug felt different from other times. He held me very tightly and I had to force my way out of the hug. I immediately told him my mother was on the phone. He came to drop something off to her so I gave him the phone. After he was done talking to her, I told her to hold on I would be right back. I showed him out and closed the door as fast as I could. I was so glad my mother was on the phone. That probably saved me from whatever he had on his mind. Both of these instances made me feel very uneasy to the point that I still remember them to this day. I knew something was not right both times and was thankful when they ended. I never felt comfortable around either one of them ever again.

Lasting Effects of Abuse and Trauma

Any of the abuses that I have mentioned above can have long lasting effects on a person. Getting professional help may be needed in order to deal with these effects. Counselors are also able to recognize abuse when it is not as apparent to the victim. Emotional and mental abuse can happen without the victim knowing what happened. Many times this abuse is so gradual it may not be noticeable. I believe that the abuse that has remained with me the longest is the mental abuse. I still hear the negative words in my mind from my mother at times when I have either made a bad decision or made a mistake. It is an uphill climb to constantly keep those thoughts is check and not let them overtake me.

Forming New Habits

One thing I am going to reference throughout this book is that we have to make new habits of how we think about and treat ourselves. Negative thoughts and feelings about ourselves created through abuse can become a habit. I believe if thoughts and feelings about ourselves linger for a long time, they represent who we are to ourselves. Once these thoughts and feelings are recognized and our desire is to rid them from our lives, it's going to take a while to make the positive thinking and feelings a habit. It may be difficult at times because the old habits have created a comfort zone for us. It has been our normal for a length of time. We have to be patient with ourselves. Science has proven that it takes a minimum of 21 days for a new habit to form. Some new habits can possibly take longer. Even as the new habit has taken shape, it is possible for the old negative thoughts and feelings to crop us at times. But it's important how we handle them. We must be careful that we don't allow those old habits to overtake us again. I feel like we have to create a new normal for ourselves. It takes time and patience on our part. DON'T GIVE UP. YOU CAN DO IT.

Someone to Listen

I have become more comfortable talking about my thoughts and feelings. Even the negative thoughts and feelings that have caused me to write this book are easier to share with others. But, and I can't stress this enough, we have to be very careful who we share those thoughts and feelings with. Just because someone is your family or friend, does not mean they are able to hear you and give you room to express your true thoughts and feelings. Many people feel it is their place to criticize us for thinking or feeling a certain way. These are definitely not the people to share with. This type of response can lead to even further wounds. The other type of response is the one who will let us vocalize a few things and then take over the conversation and make it about them. Yes they may need someone to hear them but if they are not giving us equal time, then our needs are not being met. I have experienced both types of people I trusted to hear me. I spent more time than I want to admit listening to people who only wanted to tell me how to feel and what I should do. They also liked to tell me that I should focus on the positive aspects of my situation and not the negative. I truly believed this for a long time. But when the light finally came on in my head, I was continuously contributing to invalidating my thoughts and feelings as I had before. I stopped talking to people who fit into this category. The second type of person I shared my thoughts and feelings with would allow me at least 5 minutes to talk and then take over the conversation and make it about their issues without even acknowledging anything I said. They could talk to me for 2 hours if I let them about several issues they were having. Afterwards I felt like I was drained. The majority of the time they were repeating the same thing they said to me many, many, many times before. The ideal person to share with is someone we are comfortable with, someone who genuinely cares about us and is willing to listen to us and show empathy. They listen with an understanding ear and will let you know that our thoughts and feelings matter. They allow us time and space to cry, scream and also give us a hug when we need it. The problem is we may only be able to find this person by sifting through the others. But finding them is the greatest gift. Make sure to show them appreciation. They are valuable people and should not be abused or taken for granted.

Chapter 4

Layer of Low Self-Esteem

POEM

Depart from me, those who chose to deny me myself
 those who do not understand me, or care who I am
 those who don't take the time to know
what I like and don't like
 those who think I should do it their way
 those who miss out on the authentic me, the only me that
exists and not the one who is a reflection of them to them I say I
pity you because you deny yourself the opportunity to know this
authentic me, the real me, the free me, the me who is me. I will
no longer try to be who you want me to be. I will fight to be me,
but it's been so long I have to search and find me. I spent too
much time trying to get you to like me and accept me that I lost
me. When did I lose me? What road did I leave me on and take
the detour that was the me you wanted me to be? I must go back
down the path and find my way back to the me before I became

the me of you. Will I know me when I see me or will I pass me thinking it is another me created by you?

Answering the Question

What the heck is self-esteem anyway? How do we know if it's low or high? How does it affect our life if it's low? How do we bring our self-esteem up to its normal level? What is its normal level anyway? Answering these questions can help us determine if we have low self-esteem and how to identify and deal with the causes.

One of the main causes of low self esteem is the feeling of unworthiness. Do you feel worthy of love? Do you feel worthy of a happy life? Do you feel worthy of being financially abundant? Do you feel worthy? If the answer to any of these questions is no, then low self-esteem is a byproduct.

DISCLAIMER: I'm going to put a disclaimer here. Because simply reading these questions can cause negative feelings to rise up and overtake some people. If this happens it means you have uncovered a wound that has not been healed. If you are feeling overwhelmed and need to take a step back and allow yourself time to go through those feelings, please do that. You have to be ready to allow those feelings to flow so you can get to the other side, which is healing. If you are not ready to deal with those feelings then STOP and put this book down. Take the next step and talk to a counselor or therapist. They will be able to guide you through this process.

Allowing the Pain the Flow

It took me quite a few years to allow those deeply buried feelings and thoughts to rise up in order for me to deal with them. Remember I said I started reading about this in my twenties? I am now fifty-six and still dealing with them. I wasn't able to find the strength to follow through with my healing in my twenties. I really didn't understand my wounds and even when I got close to allowing those feelings to emerge, I stopped. I wasn't able to handle going through the process of sitting with those painful memories. It wasn't until I finished seminary that I began reading material that helped me begin this journey. I had to make up in my mind that I was ready to go through the process. I knew that the only way for me to heal my life was to go through the pain.

Learning to Love Myself

I began this journey as I was reading a book by Louise Hay "How to Heal Your Life". She had a section on loving yourself. As I mentioned in Chapter 1 on Exposing the Pain, I knew that I didn't love myself but I didn't think about it much because it made me sad. But I decided to go with the flow with an exercise she suggested. It seems simple enough. She said to look into my eyes in a mirror and say "I love you, I really, really love you". So I went to the mirror in my bathroom with the full intent of accomplishing this task. As I looked into my eyes and started to say the words, I broke down. I cried uncontrollably. I could not say those simple words because I could not lie to myself. I really did not love myself. I allowed myself to feel those feelings of hurt, loneliness and unworthiness. It took me a few days but I went back to reading her book. She pointed out that many people are not able to complete this task. I was one of them. But by her understanding my pain and inability to love myself, she outlined steps to help me get to the point where I could love myself. This is one of her affirmations that helped me through this:

> *"I am worth loving. I do not have to earn love. I am lovable because I exist. Others reflect the love I have for myself."*
> https://play.google.com/store/apps/details?id=com.louise.daily

Feeling unacceptable

All my life people have told me that I am pretty, good looking or cute. But I have never felt like any of these descriptions. As a child I felt like my looks were not acceptable. As a child my mother always said I was too pale. One day she stayed home from work and she decided to put makeup on my face to "give me some color". She sent me to school at the age of 8 years old with makeup on my face. I was teased so bad my teacher told me to go into the bathroom and wash my face. I felt so humiliated. My mother didn't accept my pale face and no one else would accept the color my mother put on my face. I can't begin to tell you of the pain that experience caused me. My mother also wasn't happy with my hair. My hair was naturally wavy like my biological father's. My mother had never worked with hair like mine before. She would take me to the hairdresser who also did not know how to deal with my hair type so she pressed my hair with a hot comb and made it very straight. In the 6th grade my mother decided to put a natural wig on me and sent me to school. Of course I was laughed at and someone pulled the wig off. The laughing was uncontrollable. I didn't feel like I fit in anywhere.

A Controlling Mother

As children, we have no say so as to who our parents are. Some are kind, hard working and make sure we are loved. Some are emotionally absent, difficult to talk to and don't pay much attention to their children. Some can be cruel and treat their children like they don't matter at all.

My mother was very controlling and had no problem saying what was on her mind. She could also be mean. Remembering parts of my childhood are painful and have made it difficult for me to write at times. I wanted to be accepted by my mother and make her happy. So I did what I thought would make her happy. Sometimes it worked and sometimes it didn't. Her nickname for me was Nunu. When I got older I asked what Nunu meant. She told me it meant nuisance. Even my nickname was a source of low self-esteem.

Growing up in my house was like trying to navigate the waters. My mother was also manipulative which caused me to have to choose sides. Either I was on her side or my father's side. My father and mother never got along. They slept in separate bedrooms and their conversation was always hostile. If I spent any time with my father, she found a way to get upset with me. He was a minister and worked at Ford Motor Company. I wanted to find out more about what he did. But I was scared to spend much time with him because my mother would get upset. Choosing her side meant supporting the one who bought my clothes, food and some of the things that I wanted. When my father passed away, during the funeral many people from the church and the community gave wonderful testimonies about what a wonderful person he was. He was kind, caring and very dependable. I was angry and hurt that I didn't get the chance to know that side of my father. I lived in the same house with him and was not allowed to see who he really was.

My "godmother" also represented another person in my life who was controlling, mean, and manipulative. She always backed up my mother or even made me feel worse about myself. This upbringing caused me to doubt my thoughts and desires. I was conditioned to think that these types of people were good for my own good.

Self-sabotage

Not loving ourselves can cause us to treat ourselves badly. My dilemma in this regard is my weight. I am an emotional eater. 3 times over the last twenty years I was able to lose forty to fifty pounds. But because I didn't feel worthy to be happy

[margin note top: *choose something off my soul list? Nicola: knowing how to cope in an emotional crisis rather than picking up a Jaffa/wine for comfort*]

about my body, I ended up gaining it all back and more. Whenever something went wrong in my life, I soothed myself by eating birthday cake and drinking wine or eating cookies, bread and anything else that would make me feel good at the moment. But this type of eating also made me hate myself afterwards. This was my way of self-sabotaging. During the time while the weight was off, I kept feeling it wasn't going to last. I would see flashes in my mind of me being fat again. I would shrug it off and promise myself that I would never look like that again. But as soon as an emotional crisis occurred, all of that positive talk went right out the window. As I began this healing journey, I also realized that the times I lost the weight, I did it for the wrong reasons. I either did it to look good for someone else, to impress someone, or other external reasons probably influenced by other people. I needed to first love myself the way I was. No matter what my body looked like, I was worthy of love. This affirmation from Louise Hay was and is very helpful to me.

> "I am willing to release the need to be unworthy. I [not] am worthy of the very best in life, and I now lovingly allow myself to accept it".
> https://play.google.com/store/apps/details?id=com.louise.daily

Suppressing the Self

When our self-esteem is low we tend to allow the messages from other people dictate how we live our lives and feel about

[margin note bottom: do it for the right reasons — do it because I love myself + it's important for me to take care of my health + my life!]

ourselves. Because we don't trust ourselves we hand over control to people who think they know what is best for us. They tell us what we should wear, what we should eat, where we should work, what we should drive and who we should date. These people can come in many forms. Our parents, siblings, other family members, friends, strangers, the government, and the media have all contributed to running our life. When our self-esteem is low we will listen to everybody, anybody but ourselves. Case and point, my mother had a way of always making everything my fault. If I said to her my brother was bothering me, her response was, "just ignore him". This told me that whatever my brother did to me was my fault and not my brother's actions. My dog bit me and her response was, "if you hadn't been bothering the dog she wouldn't have bitten you". It wasn't the dogs fault it was mine. When I had my first car accident as a teenager, initially she seemed like she cared if I was injured but the next day she said, "if you had been coming home instead of dropping your friend off then it wouldn't have happened". After many years of hearing that everything was my fault, I took on that understanding which ultimately caused me to let other people off the hook for their actions. It took a long time for me to understand why I allow people to mistreat me until I remembered how my mother made me believe that everything was my fault. I have spent so much time questioning myself after a breakup because I felt it was my fault. Part of me knew that the other person played a part but my reinforced understanding that I was the cause, overshadowed it. This has been a real struggle for me. It's been fifty-seven years of thinking this way for me. I didn't understand this until I wrote this chapter.

That's why writing it has been so therapeutic for me. Otherwise I would continue to allow toxic thinking to plague my mind thereby keeping me from achieving the proper healing that I need.

I was also forced to suppress my feelings as a child. My mother always said I was too sensitive. This lowered my self-esteem as well. Being a sensitive person is one of my qualities that makes me who I am. It is not a bad thing as I was lead to believe. I had to learn that my feelings are valid and important and it's a good thing not something that should be dismissed. I am learning how to value, feel and trust my feelings. I am learning to love myself more and more everyday and allow my love to flow to others. This lets people know that I am worthy of love.

Denying the Soul's Purpose

These wounds and many more have contributed to my low self-esteem. It also caused me to bend over backwards to do whatever I could to get other people's approval. My goal in life was to please everyone. If someone got mad at me, I would think of everything I could do to make him or her happy with me again. I was the ultimate people pleaser. But I kept felling like it wasn't enough. I still didn't get treated the same way I was treating others. I still felt unaccepted. Then I read this from Louise Hay:

"If you're finding that you're saying or doing things just to appease others, then you're denying your soul's purpose."
http://www.louisehay.com/3-habits-building-self-esteem/

    I spent most of my life denying my soul's purpose. I wasn't happy because I wasn't doing what pleased me. After my second daughter left for college I was alone for the first time in thirty years. During this time I realized this was my chance to discover who I was apart from being a daughter, a wife, a mother, an employee, etc. I could finally discover me, my soul's purpose. I could finally do what I wanted to do. Then I had the greatest shock. I didn't know what I wanted. I had spent so much time doing what everyone else wanted I had lost touch with my desires. Who was I really? What made me tick? This was going to be an interesting journey but also a scary one. That was in 2011 and I was fifty years old. It is now 2018 and I'm fifty-seven. I don't have it all figured out but at least I'm not where I was 7 years ago. I can look in the mirror and tell myself "I love you, I really, really love you" every morning without hesitation. I'm learning what I like and what I don't like. I'm doing better at not trying to please everyone. It is easier for me to say no and not feel bad about it. That was a big struggle for me.

    I use to think that when I found my true self it was a chance that I would not like who I found. I now realize that is not the issue. I have realized that the sad part is that I have been in mourning for MYSELF who I was forced to give up so long ago.

My true self was stifled so much that it has taken me until now to realize what has happened. I have to continue to shed those controlling forces from my life as best I can in order for my true self to emerge. I am still on the journey and it is an uphill climb. Keeping a hold to what has already emerged is a struggle at times but I'm determined to never let go.

Chapter 5

Layer of Acceptance

Poem

      If I work hard and do my chores, she will love me.
      If I am good I will feel loved.
      If I give them what they want, they will love me.
How many times have I performed for them in search for love in return?
      The preverbal sign around my neck,
            "Will Work for Love"
was carried and acted on more times than I can recall.
I searched for acceptance and love in all the wrong places.
But how could I have known any better?

The Layer

During my lifetime I have spent an excessive amount of time looking for and working toward acceptance from people. I valued myself from their vision of me. This has been an uphill battle throughout my life because it has been difficult to please others, as we all know. Maybe I could for a time but that soon played out. After fifty-two years I finally realized what was missing, accepting myself.

As I think back on situations where the people in my life that I truly cared about and loved became distant or unresponsive to me, I spent every moment of the day running through in my mind what may have happened, what did I do, how could I have handled it better, what can I do to change the way they feel about me, how can I get them to love me more, how can I change their mind about me? The number of dialogues running through my mind I could fill several books a day. All of that time was wasted brainpower. Because when I did have a chance to talk to that person again, the words I had prepared had vanished. My brain was numb. How could I spend so much time in mental dialogue with this person but yet not be able to draw on that thinking when I needed it? This gave me another reason to ask the question, "What is wrong with me"?

Not Good Enough

I spent far too many moments feeling like I was not good enough, not smart enough, or just enough period. As a child I was led to believe that I had to earn other peoples love. So I found out what people wanted, liked, or didn't like and spent my time trying to please them so they would love me. Many times when I did something that pleased myself, it was looked at as wrong. In school I was teased if I ran a certain way, I was teased because of my name, I was teased because I was light skinned. At home my brother teased me because of the part down the middle of my head, he teased me with spiders because he knew I was afraid of them and treated me like most older brothers treated their sisters, someone who was just in the way, unimportant and unlikable. My mother was very strong willed and believed that everything she said was the truth and if you didn't agree with her, that caused a lot of discomfort around the house. My parents were older therefore they lived by the understanding that "children are to be seen and not heard". Because of this mindset, my opinion, my feelings, nor my thoughts were considered or cared about. I didn't feel loved in my house as a child so I didn't feel love for myself.

Even after I graduated from college, got married and had children, my mother made me feel like I still was not good enough. I remember going over to her house after I won an Emmy Award for the work I had done at my job. She looked at it and said, "That's nice". That is when I realized that I would never do anything good enough for her.

We ALL Need LOVE

We all need love. Every human was created in love and by the One who is love, God. So love is part of who we are. Studies have shown that a fetus is affected by the environment and attitude of the mother. If that is the case, I was longing for love before I was born. As I mentioned in chapter 3, Abandonment and Rejection, my biological mother talked about aborting me when she found out she was pregnant. Then after discussing her situation with her sister, she decided to let her adopt me. All of these conversations as I brought out in the chapter on Abandonment and Rejection, set the stage for me searching for love. My adopted mother told this story to me when I turned seventeen years old. When she told my story she told it in third person. She said she told her sister "I will take the baby". She said "the baby" instead of "I told her I would take you". She was talking to me but talked as if she were speaking about someone else.

Material support does not equal love

I don't want to sound like I was a neglected child. I was provided for with material things, food, clothing, a roof over my head and an education. People think that that equals love. How many times have we heard the phrase, "money can't buy love"? Children need more than material things for their proper development. For healthy development, a child must feel and believe that those who are the parents and or guardians of that child provide them with love. I felt like I needed to feel love from others in order to love myself. Because of this mindset, I continued to search for that love from others. I feel this is the right place to quote from the singer Johnnie Lee *"I was looking for love in all the wrong places"*.

Louise Hay helped me along this journey as well of peeling back this layer as it attributes to my parents. She said,

> *However, I Would Not Blame Our Parents for This. We are all victims of victims, and they could not possibly have taught us anything they did not know. If your mother did not know how to love herself, or your father did not know how to love himself, then it would be impossible for them to teach you to love yourself.*
>
> *Hay, Louise L. (1984-01-01). You Can Heal Your Life (p. 3). Hay House. Kindle Edition.*

Life-Liners

There were several people in my life who I would call life-liners. They threw out a life-line for me when I needed it. Because I couldn't find love at home, I searched for love everywhere else. I had play fathers and mothers at school and at church because they were people who treated me like they cared about me. They showed me kindness, understanding and listened to my thoughts. My feelings mattered, my thoughts mattered and I didn't feel like I had to do anything for them in order for me to experience that acceptance. One person who sticks out in my mind was Dr. David Snead. He was the Athletic Director at my high school. The funny thing was we looked a lot alike. After getting to know him, he allowed me to call him dad. I was his student aide during his swim class. While the students were swimming their laps, we had time to talk. He allowed me space to talk about anything that was on my mind. He gave good fatherly advice and was also very honest. My years in high school would have been very bleak if it were not for Dave. He didn't know how much I needed a father figure in my life. My adopted father was distant and emotionally unavailable. I didn't know my biological father at the time so Dave filled a void for me.

During the same time I met David, our church hired a new organist. He had so much charisma and talent it was easy to want to be around him. Dr. Stanley Waldon was this ray of sunshine for me. He was easy to talk to and allowed me space to express my thoughts. I adopted him as my big brother and he has remained my big brother for over 44 years. I knew there were times when I may have been a pest but he never treated me as if I were bothering him. He was a needed person in my life because his attention and verbal engagement was what I needed.

After high school and the end of a bad relationship, I met the man who would be my husband. Donald was also someone who allowed me space to be me, the me I knew at that time. He encouraged me to stay in school and get my degree. He introduced me to new and wonderful adventures that allowed me to get out of my comfort zone. We married after dating for 7 years and raised 2 beautiful and intelligent daughters.

After I got older I secured a job as a video editor at WXYZ Channel 7. It was a dream job but I felt intimidated by all the veteran television professionals around me and tried hard to live up to their level. Working with people I watched on television for so many years was a bit overwhelming. I tried my best to keep my uneasiness hidden. But one person helped me feel welcomed and at ease. She smiled and always spoke to me. One day she asked me about myself and genuinely cared about what I had to say. Throughout my years at Channel 7, we spent many lunch breaks talking. She always knew when something was troubling me. She always gave me a chance to talk and she listened. She was always full of compassion and understanding. During my acceptance speech when I won my Emmy Award, I said Diana Lewis was my backbone. People probably didn't understand what I meant when I said that. Diana gave me strength when I didn't believe I had strength, she supported me when I felt no once else did, she loved me when I didn't feel love anywhere else. Because of her care and support for me, I was able to have more confidence in myself and allow my light to shine. We all need life-liners in our lives. They see the person in us we need to see. They give us space to be who we are but also challenge us to grow into the person we were meant to be. They support us and give us the nudge we need to reach the next level on our journey. I thank God for my Life-Liners.

Results of an unloved self

There were several times in my adult life when I gained a lot of weight. When I was overweight, my self-esteem was lower than usual. But during the times I lost the weight I was happier with myself. But those times were short lived because my love for myself was based on what I looked like. Deep down that self-love was not there because if it was, I could love myself even when I put on the extra pounds. I love to run. After I lost the extra pounds in 2011, I was running 4 miles up to 3 times a week, lifting weights and eating the right foods. But even during this time of being the healthiest and more conditioned than I had for fifteen years, I felt something inside of myself that wanted to sabotage my progress. I recognized that thought and feeling but dismissed it. My life took a drastic turn that challenged and stressed me in ways that I had never anticipated.

- My youngest daughter left for college that flung me into the "empty nest syndrome",
- The last year of my Masters Degree was turning into my worst year,
- My oldest daughter started grad school and moved into her own apartment by herself in another state

- I gave my oldest daughter my car so I had no transportation for 4 months
- My ex-husband, the father of my daughters passed away
- My male friend ended our already fragile relationship

These life events caused me to revert back to my habit of emotional eating. What compounded my dilemma was the fact that I was living alone for the first time in twenty-three years. Since there was no one to cook for but myself, I didn't. I bought carry out food. I didn't exercise because I felt like, "who cares any way". After dealing with the stress that my school was putting me through, and keeping up with my class work and working as a chaplain intern, I had nothing left so I felt like I deserved a few glasses of wine and a huge piece of cake. But as the days added up, my well-deserved glasses of wine and cupcakes started to show up on the scale. Even though the weight was creeping back onto my hips and thighs, I was still much smaller than I was before I started losing. But the week of my graduation, I experienced a very painful episode with my sciatic nerve resulting in me walking with a cane and going to physical therapy for 3 months. Within one year, I had put all the weight back on that I had lost and then some.

Adding to the Drama

My greatest life challenge was during the time after I graduated and started working full time as a temporary university chaplain. I really wanted the job on a permanent basis but in the back of my mind those self-defeating attitudes kept creeping in. First I had to convince myself that I was capable of doing the job, and then I worked hard to prove to everyone else that I could do the job. In the midst of this challenging time of proving that I was good enough, the only thing that was stable in my life was my relationship with my daughters. I was always able to have a good conversation with my oldest daughter. Even though we didn't talk as much since she started grad school, we still had a close relationship. Or so I thought. After we celebrated Thanksgiving in 2012 she told me she had decided to leave grad school. This wasn't that bad except for the fact that this was the first time she ever made such an important decision without discussing it with me first. She had made her decision and nothing I was going to say was going to change her mind. I couldn't understand what was going on. Yes she was grown but that was totally out of character for her. Then the following week her boyfriend called and said they were going to get married at the end of December. Talking to her about this made matters worst. I felt like my whole world had just caved in. Not because of her decisions but because I felt like she no longer cared about my feelings, my thoughts or me. In hindsight, it took me back to my childhood feelings. My family did not care about my feelings, my thoughts or me. My thoughts were all over the place. What had I done wrong? Did I not love her enough? So many questions plagued my mind along with tears, prayers, anger and feeling utterly alone. I was no longer living, only existing. I felt like my heart had been ripped out and run over by a train. Going through my day-to-day activities at work and trying to keep my mind focused on my responsibilities was very difficult. My eating habits and excising had hit rock bottom. I no longer cared about myself. If it were not for my job I probably would not have left my apartment.

Spiraling out of Control

Because I struggled with self-love during my life, there have been moments that I felt like I no longer wanted to live. I never thought of taking my life but had feelings that I didn't care if I lived or died. But after I had my daughters, those thoughts would quickly be overshadowed by my love for my wonderful daughters who loved me and cared about me. That fact would always make me keep on going no matter what I was going through. But this sense of security began to unravel as my oldest daughter flexed her muscles of independence. There were times I really wanted to die because that pain was so great. I had no one who really understood my pain or even cared. I went home to an empty apartment everyday. I had a cat but she only came out of hiding when she wanted to eat. She didn't care about me either. Since I felt like no one cared, neither did I. I ate fattening foods, drank wine and ate cake. My inability to love myself was more evident than ever before. My prayers were going unanswered so I felt like God didn't care either. Yes I had friends who had stories of how their children either got married without their knowledge, or didn't marry who they wanted them to. Yes I had sympathy for their situation but this was ME, this was MY daughter who use to talk to me about everything that troubled her. We got mad together, we cried together and we discussed the different perspectives and solutions together. We went from that to this. No discussions, no shared anger, no shared tears nothing but being told what she was going to do. Unshaken, unmovable, here it is deal with it. She didn't use those words but that's what it felt like. I was shaken to my very core. After the tears dried up weeks later and I could no longer cry, I just walked around like a zombie unable to feel anything at times. Other times I felt so many different emotions that I thought I was going to lose my mind. One day it was so overwhelming, I actually heard God tell me to "get some help". I know it was God because I know it was not an idea that came from me because I was too far-gone to be that rational. After making the call I felt a bit calmer. I accepted the fact that I did need some help.

Therapy

My therapist, helped me put my life in perspective. Many things that were floating around in my mind, she was able to verbalize for me or help me verbalize them myself. My underlying problem was self-love. I was unable to maintain my weight loss because I did not love myself for who I was. If I truly loved myself, it would not go away no matter what my weight was. If I truly loved myself, I would not engage in self-defeating behaviors no matter what the stress level was in my life. If I truly loved myself, it would not go away if others did not show me the care and understanding that I felt like I deserved. Learning to love myself was of the utmost importance. It made me remember what I read months ago from Louise Hay. But I didn't continue with what I learned. My therapist also told me that I had suffered a lot of losses in my life and I needed to grieve. Loss of the old mother/daughter relationship, loss of my youngest daughter going off to college, loss of my ex-husband, etc. all accounted for my need to grieve.

Peeling Back the Layer

The main lesson I had to learn is that the love I have been searching for my entire life cannot be found in the external world from anyone or anything. The love I was searching for had to come from inside of myself. I realized that I have to love and accept myself in spite of the way other people treat me. I have to love and accept myself no matter what.

I have realized that when people do not like me, have an issue with me, or they just don't accept me for who I am, that is their problem. That is something that they need to work out within themselves. The masters, who I have read like Dr. Wayne Dyer, Louise Hay, Esther Hicks and Eckhart Tolle have helped me understand this. I am only responsible for how I feel and how I accept myself.

When we have allowed negative energy through bad thoughts, words and actions enter our life we have allowed them to take up residence within us, which goes against who god is. God is love. If we practice anything that is contrary to love, we exist outside of who we are. We are of course made in his image therefore we are love. The interesting thing is that we already know this. As Christians we read it in the bible. Other religions also understand this concept. But it is evident that this concept is not practiced on a global scale otherwise there would not be so much killing, hating and racism all over the world. We are love. It is not something we do it is who we are. But we allow the aspects of the ego (our layers) to rule us instead of our authentic soul that puts us in direct connection with our spirit that is guided by god. Many times we forget this, but sometimes we need to hear it from a different perspective in order for it to click in a way that changes us. Sometimes we say things like, let go and let god, put your burdens on the alter and leave them there, god will take care of it and many other sayings that after a while become a habit of saying words that have no meaning. If this were not the case people's life would be different. But as someone who has lived with these layers, I have put stuff on the alter but when I got up I took it back with me and those mental dialogues may have taken a break for a while, but they returned. I had to take the time and go deeper within myself and examine the layers, examine the cause of those layers and face them head on.

I Accept Myself

I acknowledge that I have to accept myself where I am at the present moment. The present moment is all that I have. The past is gone and the future does not exist yet. In his book, *"The Power of Now"*, Eckhart Tolle makes a very good point in this matter.

He says,

"Seldom do we find ourselves resting in the oceanic depth of the here and now.

For it is here - in the Now - where we find our True Self, which lies behind our physical body, shifting emotions, and chattering mind."

Tolle, Eckhart, The Power of Now, *Published August 19th 2004 by Namaste Publishing, page 6*

An out of control chattering mind is usually my problem. Whenever I was dealing with the lack of acceptance of myself it has been attributed to the chattering of negative voices in my mind. "I'm not good enough", no one loves me", what's wrong with me". But what if, we change the words in our mind from negative to positive. I started doing positive affirmations. "I love myself", I am good enough" are just some of the positive things I say especially when I am having a bad experience and that negative chatter tries to erupt in my mind. As soon as I become aware of those negative words, I stop myself and change them to my positive affirmations.

I realize that I have always tried to accept everyone for who they are except myself. I vow to work hard to accept myself no matter what other people say or do. I raised my daughters to be independent and live their lives according to their hearts desire, not the desires of others. My issues with acceptance are what lead to my downward spiral not the actions of my oldest daughter. This is what happens when we do not acknowledge our layers, the hurts that we carry within us.

At this very moment, no matter what is in my bank account, no matter what my weight is, no matter if I am in a relationship or not, no matter my job status, no matter my health situation, no matter my status in society, my acceptance of myself is crucial. I have wasted far too much time waiting until I get in shape and lose fifty pounds to accept myself. I wasted far too much time waiting until I have the right amount in my bank account to accept myself. I have wasted far too much time waiting until I'm in the right relationship to accept myself. I had to understand that I am worthy of acceptance right at this present moment. Self-acceptance is what our soul is searching for through all those layers. Far too much time is spent trying to get acceptance and acknowledgement from other people, other things and situations. That is not what our soul is longing for. Once we self accept, I believe the rest will follow.

Chapter 6

Layer of Denial

Poem

Why do you deny me who I am?
Why don't I matter to you?
Denying me causes me to deny myself
I am but a shell of a person as I deny myself for you
    No more.
      I matter
          I possess special qualities that are a part of who I am
    Recognize me
      DO NOT DENY ME
I recognize me
    I WILL NOT DENY MYSELF AGAIN

The foundation for Denial

I have spent the majority of my life allowing other people to have charge over my feelings. Instead of allowing myself to own and validate my own true feelings, I denied my pain, my sadness, hurt and denied the love I needed. I grew up believing that the love I was searching for and needed was external. As babies we come into this world as love but also required love and to be nurtured in love. When we don't receive that external love from those around us we are developmentally at a disadvantage because society reinforces this lie that the love we need and require comes from others outside of ourselves.

My childhood was my classroom for my belief that I had to work for the love of those around me. My adopted mother, Ruth was my main teacher. After I became an adult I found out from her friends that she mentioned how proud she was of me to them. I was shocked and sad to hear this because on one hand I was shocked that she was proud of me but sad because she didn't express it to me. She always made me feel like I was a disappointment and could do nothing right. I tried to do everything she wanted me to do. I didn't have much of a life as a teenager because she became very ill when I was 15 years old and other than going to school, and church, I stayed home to care for her. I wasn't the best student but I did graduate from high school and went to college. After graduating from college, I got a job and was able to purchase my own car. I got married, had children and even excelled at my job by receiving an Emmy Award for editing. None of it was good enough.

The Price of Self-Discovery

I continued to search for love to sustain me in this life from my husband and my children. My marriage fell apart when I started to discover who I was internally. I struggled with this as it weighed on my marriage. My husband was use to me going along with his opinions. But when he realized I had come into myself, his insecurities surfaced. After seeing what problems surfaced in my marriage, I tried to revert back into my old self to appease my husband. This created such discord within myself I almost lost my mind. I could not go back into that closed box I had emerged from. He was unable to make the adjustment and support the person I was growing into so we separated. My daughters were eight and twelve when we separated. They were actually relieved when he moved out because they could feel the tension between us. No matter how hard couples try to conceal their problems from their children, trust me, they can pick up on it. They may not be able to vocalize it or even know what the problem is but they know something is not right.

My children's love kept me going. They depended on me and I knew I was loved. I became sad when my oldest daughter left for college in another state but she kept in touch on a regular basis. They still depended on me. I didn't realized how much of my life was geared towards other people's dependence on me. When I think about it now, that was my reason for being for a long time, being needed and depended on by someone, anyone. When my youngest daughter left for school four years later, I had to deal with me, only me. That was the scariest time of my life.

My Feelings Matter

A few day's leading up to Mother's Day a few years after my youngest daughter left for college, I began to feel really sad. Both my daughters are away and I was alone with my dog Alaya. As I was walking Alaya that Mother's Day morning, I realized that my feelings matter, if to no one else, they matter to me. I had a rush of memories of people in my life, especially those who said they loved me and cared about me, tell me that my feelings and thoughts about a situation were wrong and that their thoughts and feelings were more important than mine. My feelings were dismissed and disregarded. As this ran through my mind I realized that what they thought and felt was their way of supporting them and their agenda. They were cherishing their feelings and ignoring mine. Because I was raised unable to cherish my feelings or thoughts, it was now time for me to do so. During my walk with Alaya, I realized that if I continue to deny my feelings, I just add to the long list of people who discount my feelings as well. I can no longer sell myself out. I have to cherish my feelings even if no one else does. I've done this for far too long. Every time I allow someone else to shut me down because I have expressed my feelings on a situation, I have to cherish those feelings that are within me. I cannot ignore them nor deny them. If I do, I am denying myself and showing them that their feelings are more important than mine. Just as their feelings are important to them, my feelings are important to me. Even if we disagree, everyone's feelings should be cherished and not shut down. If we allow other people to shut down our feelings and treat us like that part of us does not matter, we are allowing them to tell us that we don't matter. When we allow this to happen, we deny ourselves. This is another layer covering up our soul.

As I mentioned earlier, looking for love and acceptance externally from other people will keep us acquiring the love that we actually need. The love we really should search for is inside of ourselves. Love is not an emotion but it is a way of being. As I read messages on Facebook after coming in from walking my dog, I found a quote from Eckert Tolle that speaks to this fact. He said,

> *"Love is a state of being. Your love is not outside; it is deep within you. You can never lose it, and it cannot leave you. It is not dependent on some other body, some external form. In the stillness of your presence, you can feel your own formless and timeless reality as the unmanifested life that animates your physical form. You can then feel the same life deep within every other human and every other creature. You look beyond the veil of form and separation. This is the realization of oneness. This is love."*
> **Eckhart Tolle, The Power of Now.**
> https://www.eckharttolle.com/special/love/

We are led to believe that love is an action but love is actually a way of being. Many who believe in God and the writings in the Bible know the scripture that states we were "*created in the image of God*". We also know the other scripture that says, "*God is Love*". As I look at these two scriptures, it says that we are love. We are made in the image is God and that image is love. "Is" does not fit into the category as an action word but as a state of being. Since love is who we are, we have to take the time to search within ourselves for the love we yearn for.

External Love reinforced

My journey inward has been a sometimes-difficult one because the old habits of the search for that external love resurfaces from time to time and I end up in a tug of war between the two. Society is constantly at work to reinforce this concept of external love. It not only tells us that we need love from other people it also tells us we can find that needed love from things. Television, the internet, the government and people in our lives show us every minute of the day how money, power, cars, games, jewelry, boats and many other "things" can give us a momentary sense of satisfaction but it pales to compare to the real, sustaining love that our soul longs for.

Understanding that true love comes from within has helped me tremendously. Reading works from Dr. Wayne Dyer, Eckert Tolle and many others has not only brought out a stronger meaning of key Biblical scriptures to me but introduced me to other readings and authors who have over come their search for external love and found and understood the love from within. Expanding the reality and understanding of love from within is critical for each and every one of us. Once the love is discovered and nurtured from within, we are able to express that genuine love to others in a whole new way.

During a conversation with my oldest daughter, we were talking about the importance of forgiveness. I talked about needing to still be able to forgive my adopted mother. I said that maybe I should think about the positive things she did for me, like the things she bought for me and did for me. My daughter said "mom that is not the way I think you should deal with that. I think you need to be real with your feelings and how she really made you feel". She was right. Her statement hit me like a ton of bricks. In denying my true feelings about my adopted mother, I was doing the same thing to myself that she did to me by denying my feelings and thoughts. I have been denying my true feelings and thoughts about her to try and find a way to sugarcoat it by focusing on the materialistic things she did for me. I can no longer deny myself. As a child my feelings and thoughts were denied and treated like they didn't matter, I didn't matter. I grew up with this same mindset. It is time to take me back. It is time for me to own my thoughts and feelings and never, never, never allow anyone to deny me, myself again.

The work must continue

Even after consciously working on this layer for several years, I still find areas that need attention. It can be exhausting at times, emotionally, mentally and spiritually, but the journey is better than sitting in a lake of stagnation that will get me nowhere.

Each person is unique. Our thoughts, our likes and dislikes, our various perspectives and our layers make us unique. It's time to stop denying who you are. If you ask the question, "who am I" because you have been lost from yourself for so long that you do not know, then venture out on the journey of self discovery. Yes it can be a scary journey. Anytime we venture out into the unknown, it can be scary. But your discovery will not be into the unknown, it is actually a journey into rediscovering who you are. You have always been there just covered up by the layers of discontent.

Chapter 7

The Layer of Anger

Poem
The switch is on and my anger grows with each thing that goes wrong
This printer wont work right - I can't find a job - Everybody hates me
I hate me
Why can't things just work right
Why am I cursed - I just want to die - Why am I here
Now my car won't start
What, why, God why do you hate me
I'm getting madder and madder
Come on car why won't you start (sobbing uncontrollably)
It hit you for not starting - oh the pain, the pain in my hand - it won't stop hurting,
I'm bleeding - I can't move my hand
What did I do

Anger, Fear, Loneliness, unworthiness, despair now a broken hand

Reaching My Boiling Point

Anyone will tell you that I am not an angry person. I am pretty easygoing and calm but I have on occasion been sad and very unhappy during my life. But there are times over the years during struggling times, that I get angry when I have been working hard to keep things going. On those days when everything seems to go wrong, I get frustrated first as I keep trying unsuccessfully to make something work. One day I had a moment of frustration when my printer refused to work after I tried everything. I am a technical person and this was not supposed to happen to me, right? After working with this printer for over an hour, that anger switch came on and I snatched it off the desk and walked to the stairs and, yes you guessed it, threw it down the stairs. There, take that you stupid printer. As I stood there I could feel my angry level diminish and turn into regret. I started crying over my frustration of getting that angry and now I don't have a printer. I also have to clean up this mess and throw it away before my daughters come home. I don't want them to know I got angry enough to throw a printer down the stairs.

Anger gone Too Far

There were a few over times I got that angry but one time I let it go way too far. After I didn't get the job as the associate chaplain at Northwestern University, I couldn't find another job so I started taking seminary classes again to finish a second master's degree. I could survive for a while on the scholarships and financial aide and also pick up a few hours as an on call chaplain. But during the summer, there was no financial aide or scholarship money. So, after trying everything else I could think of, I needed to apply for foods stamps so me and my daughter, who was home from school for the summer, would be able to eat. People who work at the food stamp office can be cold and totally uncaring for the person who has to ask for assistance. I know they have a lot of people to meet with, but from the other side of the situation, it is very aggravating to show up 30 minutes early for my appointment and still be kept waiting for 3 hours. I brought all the needed information I was asked to bring. Of course the thing they did not ask for, my caseworker wanted. After driving to both my less than part time jobs to get this information, I had to go to a printing service to make copies and fax them back to my caseworker. I didn't have enough money on my debit card so I went home to see if I had enough money to purchase a kiosk card. I found the money and drove back to the printing store and went in to purchase a card only to find out that the machine had no kiosk cards. By this time I was so disgusted. I had to fax these papers to my caseworker within the next 20 minutes. It was a Friday and the clock was ticking. I was going to go home to call a friend and see if they could fax my sheets from their fax machine. I went back to my car, feeling so defeated. I got into my car, put the key into the ignition and it would not turn. My key literally would not turn. I tried to turn the steering wheel just in case it was a little off but it still would not turn. I tried everything. The more I tried, the angrier I got. I tried for 20 minutes to get this key to turn. I even got on the passenger seat and tried. Nothing. I went back to the drivers seat and kept trying. As the tears flowed, my heart pounded, and I just wanted to hit something. I tried to hit the steering column but missed and hit the end of my key. This was a metal key with no plastic coating. I hit pure metal. OMG the pain was horrible. I tried to shake it off but it would not stop hurting. I looked at the spot on my hand where I hit and it had a little hole in it and blood was coming out. Blood was dripping onto my pants and my seat. O God what had I done? Now I can't use my hand. How do I get home? What am I suppose to do, I shouted to God. I had to use my left hand to continue trying to start my car and guess what, it started. WHAT THE HELL? I was in a lot of pain as I drove home. What was I going to tell my daughter? I got so mad I broke my hand. That is so embarrassing and humiliating. I never want my daughters ever to think that I'm a looser. That's what I felt like. I sat in my car after parking in front of my apartment feeling grateful that I my car started and I was able to get this crazy thing home. But now I have to deal with my hand. As if I don't have enough to deal with now I may have broken my hand. I don't think I have ever felt so worthless.

My daughter was so worried about me when I walked through the door as she looked at my hand. Through the tears and pain that shown on my face, I had to tell her what happened. She prompted me to go to the hospital. She didn't have her license so I called a friend in my building to drive me to the hospital. The doctor told me that it was broken. I felt so, for lack of a better word, stupid. This was a very dark time for me so my descriptions of myself were not good. Now the few hours I was working at my school as a video editor were no longer possible. I also can't drive, so I can't even work my on call chaplain hours. So what little money I was making was now going to stop.

It is a very difficult decision for me to make when I am forced to apply for unemployment or food stamps. To realize that I have to reach out for that help, is admitting that I am unable to provide for myself and my family. Accepting this mindset was admitting failure to me. And given that when I do go through this process and enter into these places where I have to wait 4 hours for a rude person to humiliate me even further, it adds to the depletion on my humanity.

A Child's Anger

My youngest daughter had anger issues as a toddler. I couldn't understand why she was so angry. My husband, my oldest daughter and I showed her great amounts of love. But I came across an article that said the mother's moods and anxiety can be transferred to her unborn child while she is pregnant. I became very sad because while I was pregnant with her I was very distressed and sad most of the time. First my adopted father passed away when I was 5 months pregnant. But what was worse, my adopted mother, Ruth and my godmother, enjoyed saying hurtful and demeaning things to me. I was also sleep deprived because I worked a 4am shift at my job. All of this caused a lot of stress in my life on a regular basis. My sadness turned into anger after I thought about what my mother and godmother put me through. They knew I wouldn't say anything back to them as they ridiculed me on a regular basis. My oldest daughter, stayed with Ruth while I was at work. When I went to her house to pick up my daughter, as soon as I saw my godmother's car, I knew what I would have to endure when I walked inside. My godmother made my Ruth's attitude toward me even harsher. Neither one of them had anything positive to say about me; it was always negative and judgmental.

    Over the years, I have been able to keep those thoughts from invading my mind for the most part until I talked to my youngest daughter about her struggles with anxiety. When she was a toddler and expressed so much anger, I decided to get her to laugh every time she got angry. It worked and I thought all was well. But as I have expressed throughout this book, those wounds, hurts and emotional scars don't just go away. Some of them are "trapped emotions" that need special attention. My daughter is dealing with general anxiety issues possibly because of those early feelings of anger we couldn't understand. After she told me this, I went back in my thinking to try to figure out where it came from. As a mother I asked myself the usual questions, *"what did I do to cause this"?, "how could I have protected her better?", "what could I have done differently?".* As I began to relax and stop beating up on myself, it hit me. The anxiety and depression I suffered with when I was pregnant with her as well as the way in which my mother treated my daughters when they were at her house all play a part in her anxiety.

Resolving My Anger Issues

Breaking my hand was a serious wake up call for me. I allowed my anger to actually cause physical injury, cause me to think and feel worse about myself, put me in a worse financial situation and made me look really bad to my daughter. Everything I was trying so hard to correct and change in my life just got worse. I would say that practicing meditation, (still working on doing it on a regular basis), saying affirmations, or other mind calming techniques has helped with my anger issue which they have, but the greatest thing that has helped me is remembering what happened the last time I got angry, a broken hand. Yes my life has gotten better, but the main thing is my attitude towards myself has gotten better. I have learned how to be more grateful for what I have and the wonderful people in my life. But loving myself more is the most important part. If your anger get's the best of you, work on self-love and being more grateful. Try meditation and affirmations to help to calm your mind. Being angry only hurts, it doesn't help.

Chapter 8

The Layer of Fear

POEM

I live with memories that can stunt my growth.
　Why did she?　　Why did he?　　Why did they hurt me?
　Why didn't she?　Why didn't he? Why didn't they love me?
I get so tied up with those thoughts from the past that the life I was put here to live is a distant reality. If that wasn't bad enough, the time I do free up from thoughts of the past, I spend it fearing the future.
　How will I?　　What will happen if?　　What if they don't?
These questions plague my mind and keep me tied up in mental bondage.
　It's time to break free and live in the present moment. The present moment, right now is all there is.
　The past is gone. It no longer exists.
　The future is not hear, it doesn't exist yet.
I have to stop wasting my time in the not now and live in the right now.

Fear is a choice

Fear as a By-Product

Fear can be the by-product of all the other layers that cover the soul. Abandonment, rejection, trauma and abuse, secrets and lies can create a sense of fear in forming relationships with others as well as creating the fear of making decisions within myself. Because of my many years of feeling abandoned, and rejected, there is a fear within me of having these experiences again. Many times because of fear, we can subconsciously sabotage our relationships before they turn bad in order to avoid being abandoned and rejected. Fear can also be a byproduct of trauma and abuse. Depending on the abuse and the abuser, sometimes starting or maintaining relationships can be difficult. In my case I am very conscious now of my actions in my past relationships. I am very choosy as to who I am in a relationship with but when I am in one; I tend to do things that sabotage them. I have in the past been needy or clingy while loosing myself to please him. Of course I choose men who don't deal well with either one of these qualities so they end the relationship. Now weather it would have ended for other reasons is also possible but my actions were the same in each case. Always in the back of my mind was the fear that they would end the relationship. I did everything I could think of to stay in their good favor but they may have been the wrong things. I studied all kinds of relationship techniques, read all kinds of relationship books all telling me what I was doing was wrong. But making myself do the opposite was very difficult. I kept feeling like I was not being me. I was right. I now understand that I need some healing to take place within me so self-sabotage is no longer feels normal.

Fear of Failure or maybe Success

I have put off doing things that could possible be the best thing for myself because I was afraid of failure or maybe it's a fear of success. I'm not sure which one it is. I spend too much time wondering and analyzing. This book is a prime example. I have been working on it off and on since 2013. I know one reason is because it's healing for me and that it has brought up some difficult emotions that have caused me to step away from writing several times for periods of months at a time. But I cannot ignore the reality of the fear attached to it as well. What if no one will buy it? What if no one likes it? What if someone gets mad at me for something I have written? What if they do like it and want me to talk about it? What if they want me to write another book? What if, what if, what if? I can't tell you how much time I have wasted with these "what if" fears. But I keep coming back to it. That's progress.

Getting out of my comfort zone has been a fear of mine for years. Another time in my life where I forced myself to get out of my comfort zone and face my fears was when I left my full time job, moved out of my house and moved myself and my daughter to Evanston, Illinois to attend seminary. Many people thought I was crazy. Heck, I thought I was crazy but there was this force within me, pushing me. As I sat waiting for orientation to begin, I was so scared I felt like a kid waiting outside the principles office. Would I be able to do graduate work? I haven't been in school for at least 20 years. My God I'm 48 years old. What have I done? All of these questions plagued my mind. But as I looked around, the majority of the students in orientation were around my age or older. This meant that I was not the only one who stepped away from a career in search of a new direction. That brought me some comfort. After a while it felt good to have stepped out of my comfort zone. This was one of many times I faced my fears and was able to grow in many areas of my life.

A Big Change and a Huge Challenge

I faced with a huge challenge. My oldest daughter and her husband were moving to the UAE to teach. They wanted me to join them and take care of my only grandchildren while they work. I agreed because I wanted to be a part of my granddaughter's lives. I wanted them to not only have a lot of memories of me but a lot of great memories. Relocating to the UAE was exciting and scary. My job cut my hours and I need a change. I was ready for a new adventure and a chance to make some positive changes in my life. But my challenge was leaving my youngest daughter in America. Her sister and me are the ones who she can always depend on. My youngest daughter could get on a bus or train and visit us when things became too overwhelming or just wanting to spend time with us. Now both her sister and me were going to be on the other side of the world.

I want her to go with us but she wants to stay. My other strong independent daughter doing what she feels is right for her. I feel really good that I raised 2 strong, independent women. It was difficult for me during this transition but I'm learning how to be a mother to grown women.

To be honest, I was scared and overwhelmed as I thought about moving to another country. I had to get rid of most of the things in my apartment or put it in storage. I had so much on my mind I felt like I was going to lose it. I had those "what if" questions that bombarded my mind. But my main concern was for my wonderful dog, Alaya.

Leaving my Dog

My other fear was leaving my awesome dog Alaya. She was more like a therapy dog for me. After both my daughter's were away at college, I had to learn how to deal with being alone. It was very difficult. During my youngest daughter's sophomore year she talked me into getting a puppy. After much reluctance and seeing the picture of this cute little yellow lab, I was hooked. Alaya helped me through some of the most difficult moments of my life. When I felt like I had no one who gave a damn, Alaya showed me compassion, love and care. As I sat and cried because I felt so lost, Alaya would lay her head on my chest. She would even lick the tears from my face. Those moments gave me new life. She helped keep me going. Many times I didn't know where I was going but we went together. My challenge was that I had to leave my wonderful companion behind. I didn't have the money to fly her over in a way I know she would be safe and properly taken care of. I had to find her a new home. This tore me up inside.

Alaya the Lifesaver

Alaya has saved my life several times. I say this because there were times when things were so bad I just didn't want to live any more. The pain was too great. The thought of stepping in front of a speeding truck on the freeway crossed my mind a few times as I lived with my half sister. Stopping the pain with an overdose of pills and going to sleep and never waking up again seeped into my mind. But as I looked into Alaya's eyes, I felt unconditional love and it brought me back every time. I've had many dogs throughout my life but this dog has been not only my favorite but she was also a therapist when I needed it. I could talk about my frustrations and she listened and then licked my face as if to say, "everything will be ok".

Not only was Alaya a lifesaver she also had the great ability to make me laugh even when I don't feel like it. I had been working in the television industry off and on for over 30 years. I've been a news editor, and then a stagehand before I moved. Working at a news station, I am surrounded by negative input. Killings, kidnappings, stabbings, shooting, you name it, we had it. After going to seminary and then studying spirituality and metaphysics, it tries my sanity when I go to work. It worked against everything I've been trying to do to give me a more positive attitude. The fear that I was working to get out of my life, has seeped it's way back in. But coming home after listening to all the bad news of the day, Alaya was always eager to see me walk through the door. She was my welcome home party every day. She licked me and jumped on me and showed me unconditional love. No questions, no complaints, just love. I had to find someone who would love her as much as I do. I see so many pictures of dogs being mistreated. It would just rip me apart if anyone did that to my Alaya. I was afraid I wouldn't be able to find someone to take her before I left. The very thought of having to take her to a shelter caused my heart to break.

Change is Scary

I have always looked forward to change during my life. Small minor changes are not as scary as the big ones. This one was huge. It was scary when I left my job and moved to another state to attend seminary full time. But this move was much scarier. Moving to another country is not like a move across the USA. It's a different culture, different rules and I'm going to be a visitor and not a citizen.

Fear as a way of Life

The media, the government, social media and society as a whole make fear a large part of our life. Crime, identity theft, financial problems and war are saturating the news on a daily basis. If we don't watch the news on television, we will see it on social media, glance at a newspaper headline or it is portrayed in television shows and movies. How can we escape this fear? Dr. Wayne Dyer says it best.

> *Fear is present when we forget that we are a part of God's divine design. Learning to experience authentic love means abandoning ego's insistence that you have much to fear and that you are in an unfriendly world. You can make the decision to be free from fear and doubt and return to the brilliant light of love that is always with you. Who you really are is that unclouded love.*
>
> http://www.drwaynedyer.com/blog/move-back-to-love/

Faith vs Fear

Many people of faith live a conflicted life. I say this because I'm one of them at times. Fear cannot exist if one has faith. The Bible talks about faith in many areas. First of all having faith is a gift given by God (Ephesians 2:8-9). Some people reading this may not believe in God. That does not change the fact that He is real and without Him we would not exist. Even though I know this, I still experience fear at times. How can I have faith and experience fear as well? See the conflict? I mean, hey I went to Seminary, I should have it all figured out by now right? Being a Christian does not mean that we are perfect and that negative stuff has been banished from our mind and our heart. As with everything in life it is a journey. I'm on this road too not only be a better Christian but to be a better Annette. I'm on a journey to connect with The God inside me who loves me unconditionally, guides me, gives me peace and provides healing for all the layers I'm dealing with. But there is one main thing that I must do. I must give up control. When I allow fear to take hold of me and cause me to sabotage relationships, I am in control. When I allow abandonment and rejection to plague my mind, I am in control. When I allow my past traumas and emotional and mental abuse to send me into depression, I am in control. I say I'm in control because I choose to think those thoughts instead of allowing the God in me to bring me peace and change my way of thinking. Slowly this is taking place. I have more peace in my life and I am not as fearful as I use to be.

Let us not be so hard on ourselves. If fear is what is present in our lives, let us admit it. But let us not stop there. Pray or meditate on what in our lives we can be grateful for. Let's spend five minutes a day thinking about only what we have to be grateful for. After a week, add another five minutes and every week after that add five more. Every minute we spend feeling grateful are minutes where fear does not exist.

I want to end with this statement from an e-book I read.

> *Your True Self is fearless, loving, and totally free. Realizing its unlimited life as your own enables you to enter a whole new world within yourself whose very ground is the unshakable strength, security, confidence, and contentment you were born to know.*
> http://151affirmations.com/free-affirmations-ebook-download/

Chapter 9

The Layer of Trust

Poem

How can I ever trust again?

I've been used and abused and they made me believe they loved me.

My heart has been stepped on so many times

I don't know if it even works any more.

I trusted because I cared. Who can I trust with my heart?

My trust belongs with God. He knows and will heal.

I can depend on Him who works His miracles in me.

I can trust me as long as I have Him.

Who Can I Trust?

Living with the various layers from the previous chapters and some I have not focused on can cause serious trust issues with people. Experiencing these hurts and disappointments over and over again will unleash an overwhelming distrust of those who hurt us as well as those who have not hurt us. We build a wall that keeps people from getting too close to us. We are so tired, so sick and tired of feeling that hurt and being disappointed that we promise ourselves that no one will hurt us again. We begin doing everything ourselves. We ask no one for help and we do not accept assistance from anyone. We do not love anyone fully and do not allow anyone to get close enough to love us. We either cope by having sex with no feelings attached or shut down all together and have no intimate contact for fear of those feelings rising up once again. We wear ourselves out living in this mindset because we always have to be on guard.

During my years as a teenager, I really didn't have anyone to depend on except for the basics of living, which I was grateful for. But when it came to supporting me in the things that made me happy or things I was interested in, I could not trust that anyone from my family would be there for me. If it was something that my mother wanted me to do, then she was there. I loved sports as a teenager. I was on the swim team, I played tennis, I played volleyball, basketball, softball and ran track. No one from my family ever came to see me play. I just got use to it after a while and stopped looking for anyone to support me. I had to be self motivated. Many parents don't realize how important it is to support their children. Support shows children they are important and what they care about matters. It helps to validate them and let them know they are loved and supported. It still causes me pain as I type these words remembering how alone I felt in my own family. I felt like no one cared about those things that were a part of who I was. It was plain to me that what I cared about was not worth supporting. I didn't realize that this was still hurtful until I stared writing this chapter. But I know that I need to let these feeling go so they can heal. But I have to recognize that pain and allow it to flow before healing can begin. As I stated before, that layer must be peeled away. That is why I am continuing to type as tears flow down my cheeks because this is the only way I can heal. I have to allow myself to go through this pain in order for it to go away once and for all. It may take a while but I have started the process. I will not allow myself to run from this pain any longer. It has taken up too much of my life already.

Determined to be Different

I learned from this experience that I would make time to support my children in everything they cared about. There were very few soccer matches, golf events and concerts I missed for my two daughters. I took vacation days and even called in sick so I would not miss my daughters performances. I always wanted to let them know that I was there for them and that what they cared about also mattered to me. I remember how devastated I was when I thought I would not be able to attend my oldest daughters senior vocal concert before she graduated from college. I was in seminary and was not working so I didn't have the money to drive from Illinois to Kentucky for her concert. My youngest daughter and I went to visit her a month earlier and one of her friends was giving her senior recital. So the thought of me attending her friend's recital and not my daughters was crushing to me. As I told my daughter about my dilemma, she said "that's OK momma". That make me feel even worst because it took me back to my days of my mother not being in attendance for something that was important to me and I just cried my eyes out as I sat alone immersed in despair. As her performance got closer, I decided to pawn my laptop to get the money I needed to drive to Kentucky. I'd get the money somehow to get my laptop back. The only thing that was important at that moment was to be sitting in the audience to hear my baby give her final recital as an undergraduate. I wanted my daughters to always trust that I would be there for them no matter what. I wanted them to trust that I would always support them and care about what they cared about.

    I never guarded my heart when it came to my daughters. They were really the only ones I didn't have to do that with. Of course we had our ups and downs but nothing to the point where my heart was crushed.

    I stretched outside my comfort zone by attending seminary. I had to let down my wall of trust a bit in order to take classes and put a certain amount of trust into professors, administration and my fellow students. For 2 ½ years, things were going well. I was getting really good grades, my professors were good and I had found new friends. I was comfortable in my surroundings.

That wall of distrust was coming down quite a bit and I was feeling good.

Another Challenge

I was entering my last year in seminary as my oldest daughter began her first year in grad school in Kentucky and my youngest daughter began her undergrad career. I had turned 50 years old at the beginning of the year. I had a lot going on but had been successful in exercising on a regular basis, eating right, which resulted in trimming down from 220 pounds to 175. I felt great. I hadn't felt or looked this great in years. I was running 4 miles 3 times a week. Whenever I would get stressed about anything I went out and started running. This was the best stress reliever I knew. But in the fall, things began to unravel. I was dealing with the "Empty Next Syndrome". The man I was spending time with and who I thought was going to spend more time with me since I was now alone, decided that he wasn't ready for a relationship with me after all. The next thing that happened was my ex-husband passed away. This devastated my daughters. They were both away at school and I had to tell them over the phone. That hurt me to my soul. Then my seminary professors decided to throw a wrench in my last year and forced a last minute integrative paper in our lap with vague instructions. Since their directions were so scattered, each professor graded from their own understanding. I ended up with the two worst professors to read my paper. They failed my paper not once but twice. After 3 years of getting nothing but A's and 2 B's on all of my Master's level papers, this was a devastating blow. In the midst of all of this, I took my car to my oldest daughter. Her apartment was 5 miles from campus and her schedule ended pretty late at night because of rehearsals. I didn't want her trying to figure out how to get home so I took her my car. I rode my bike everywhere I went or took the train. When it got cold as it does living on Lake Michigan in Illinois, I was unable to get to the gym on a regular basis. So being able to run when I got stressed did not happen during a time when I really needed it. That final integrative paper almost drove me crazy. Also my school decided to reject my proposal for a cross-cultural experience so I was also stressing about that. It was April and I was supposed to graduate in May. Finally I got a call from the registrar's office and was told that I had taken a class that fulfilled my cross-cultural requirement. What a relief. 3 days before I graduated, I had a sciatic attack for the first time in my life. I had to walk with a cane for 4 days. But I graduated and passed my final paper. That was over. But I didn't want to leave this community. I was working as a chaplain at the chapel at Northwestern University and truly enjoyed what I was doing. As I got more and more comfortable with my wall of distrust coming down, I was asked to replace the outgoing Associate Chaplain until they found a permanent replacement. It was a huge challenge for me. I had to really get out of my comfort zone to do this. I doubted myself at first, but convinced myself I could do a good job. I also applied for the permanent job. I figured I've been an intern for 2 years and doing the job for a year, I knew the students and the chapel community, I was a good choice. I busted my butt every day proving that I could do this job. In the midst of this particular year, my oldest daughter decided she was going to drop out of grad school and give up a full scholarship. "A full scholarship" I thought she has lost her mind. We talked, yelled, and argued like we had never done before. This was the daughter who I could talk to about anything. Whenever she had a problem, (or so I thought) she knew she could come and talk to me as she had done many, many times before. After a few hours engaging in this argument, I decided to back down. After all she had been going to school every year since pre-K non-stop without a break. I figured it would be all right for her to take a break. After all she had lost her father and dealt with a medical issue. She deserved a break. Then a few days later I received a call from her boyfriend who I have only met once, telling me that he and my daughter were going to get married the end of the month. I almost lost my mind.

I know that this was a long scenario but it was necessary to lead up to the point I want to make about trust. I trusted that my daughters would love me and respect me the same way I did them. I trusted that they would communicate with me about all important matters. As a mother I was supposed to help my daughter plan her wedding. I tried to talk my daughter out of what I thought was a crazy idea. She hadn't finished her Masters degree, he hadn't finished his undergrad so what was the rush? She wasn't pregnant so why couldn't they wait until they both graduated? I tried to get our pastor to talk to her, friends and relatives but she decided against it. As a result, they were going to get married no matter what I said. I trusted my daughter with my heart and it was breaking. I felt like a guest at her bridal shower and at her wedding. I felt out of place and that I really didn't matter to anyone. I just wanted to die. I felt like my heart was ripped out of my chest and run over by a semi truck. Thank God I was not taking classes or I would have failed miserably. After getting home I just functioned every day not living at all. After work, my dinner consisted of a big square of cake from the grocery store and a half bottle of wine. All the weight I had lost the previous year I gained back and more. I watched reruns of detective shows and cried myself to sleep. One day as I just existed, I couldn't watch television any more, I couldn't read anything and being alone made me even more depressed. Then the voices started going off in my head. Voices of all the negative things people have said to me my whole life. My mother's voice, my brother's voice, my husband's voice, negative teachers, old boyfriends and many other negative things said to me over my life time. I felt like I had just dropped into the deepest, darkest hole ever and I couldn't get out. Then after 30 minutes of this I heard another voice tell me "get some help". I listened and went to the Internet and found a therapist and send her an email and told her I needed to see her.

After making the appointment, I began to feel a little better. The negative voices were dying down. During my appointment with my therapist, Alyse Rynor, helped me realize that I have to be responsible for my own happiness and the kind of trust I put in others was not healthy. That kind of trust is susceptible to disappointment every time. It took me a few months but after I began to heal from those hurts I suffered during my ordeal with

my daughter, I realized that I had raised my daughters to be independent. I told them not to let anyone tell them how to live their lives and to live out their dreams. My daughter was doing what I trained her to do. Even though I thought what she was doing was a mistake, it was her life and I needed to respect that and trust that she knew what was best for her.
After all, it was not my life, it was hers. So I had to make the adjustment and allow her to be the grownup that I raised her to be. I didn't want my daughter to lose her trust in me like I had lost.

While I was learning how to trust in a different way, I encountered a situation that challenged that newfound trust before I could get use to it. It was a situation at my seminary. After I didn't get the permanent chaplain's job, I began working on another master's degree in counseling. As a student worker at my school, someone who I considered a friend and respected as a leader and scholar challenged and questioned my sanity. She tried to manipulate me make me think that I was on the verge of a breakdown. I left that conversation confused. The confusion turned into anger. "How dare she question my sanity." "How dare she." I was furious. Should I report her, should I tell her how wrong she was, should I sock her in the face? I wanted to do all those things but what will I gain? That would be totally out of character for me and would let her know that she could get to me. I prayed very, very hard and was able to stop working in her office and get a part time job elsewhere.

I realize that the trust I need is trust in myself. My intuition was sending me signals in each situation that something wasn't right and I needed to look at it from a different perspective or be on alert. That little voice we hear telling us what to do is the voice we need to listen to. Listening to this voice can help us from much heartache and pain. Think about it. How many times have we said, I should have listened to that little voice, I should have listened to my first choice. I know I have done this so many times in my life. But it felt so good to ignore that voice and do what I wanted to do after much deliberation and excuses as to why I need to do it the other way. Be careful how much trust you put in others. Instead let's love and trust ourselves more.

Chapter 10

The Layer of Forgiveness
POEM

In my alone time I wonder what it is that is holding me back. Why do I feel stuck in my self-discovery? Why aren't my dreams coming true, where is my breakthrough?

I can't shake the feeling that you have something to do with my stagnating. Did you teach me what I needed to know to make the best of myself, or did you hinder my development? What part did you play in my ability to be all I can be?

I read that forgiveness is the key to unlocking the door to the freedom of self that has been locked away from my grasp.

Forgive?
        Forgive You?
How can I forgive you for what you did to me?
I'm still angry with you but you are not here to make it right. Even if you were here, would your apology be enough?
        There must be a better way.

I read somewhere that
   "Un-forgiveness is like taking poison and waiting for the other person to die".
   I must release this hold you have over me.
Not forgiving you is my burden - not yours.
You are dead.   I want to live.   I have to forgive you.

The Need to Forgive

As with my other layers, this one is not peeled back completely. This one is especially challenging because the things that I feel were done to me caused the other layers to exist. Because of the rejection that was projected upon me with the discussion of aborting me produced the feelings of abandonment. My childhood produced the idea that I was not worthy of love because it was something I had to earn by being good, doing my chores, being the perfect little girl. We all know that there are no children in existence like this so what I was expected to be was unreasonable. Because of this situation that was planted in my understanding, the love, the genuine love that all children desire was withheld. Even after I became an adult, my accomplishments and even awards were not good enough. Needless to say this took care of the mental and emotional layers that covered my soul. The low self-esteem layer took hold as well as I tried to navigate through my childhood searching for acceptance. As I grew into an adult, I got mental flashes of the patterns I was living over and over again in my relationships but I kept denying what was right in front of me. The anger inside me grew and I didn't know why. Every time I became angry, all the other feelings came up as well. The fear, the rejection, the self-hatred, all paraded through my mind and took me from anger to depression.

Healing the Scars

Allowing the scars to heal that my adopted mother left in me has been a hard fought battle. If I screwed up something she told me I was "hamscammy". It was a word she made up meaning that I was a screw up. I have heard this word float through my mind when I did something wrong as an adult. Before I began this road of healing and self-discovery, I heard this word often and it made me feel like a screw up. It would almost paralyze me.

I remember to this day when my mother put makeup on me as a child and sent me to school because she said I was too pale. I also remember that my hair was not right for her because she didn't know how to deal with wavy hair. So she would press it very straight. She said I was too sensitive. It was like everything that made me who I was as a person was wrong. I read an article on the website, www.justorganicmedicine.com and it speaks to this very point. It states,

"Our mother's and father's voice is something that gets integrated deeply into our psyche, it becomes our inner voice. **The way they speak to us becomes the way our inner voice speaks to us, the way we speak to ourselves.** *If they are angry most of the time they speak to us, if they are harsh and cold, if they shout and yell whenever we do something wrong, that's how we'll deal with ourselves whenever we make a mistake."*

http://justorganicmedicine.com/psychologists-warn-never-use-these-5-phrases-when-talking-to-your-child/

My Growing Anger

Feeling ignored, unloved and unimportant by my mother has caused me to have difficulty in forgiving her. Realizing that all of the negative things that I have been telling myself my whole life started as things that were said to me as a child. I have been angry with her for a long time. Not only did she treat me this way, she treated my daughters the same way. My husband and I traveled to West Africa with our church for ten days. My daughters stayed with my mother while we were gone. I missed them so much but the one thing that kept me going was that when my husband and I walked through the door, our 2 beautiful daughters would run to us and give us huge hugs like they always did. This time I knew the hugs would be more meaningful because we had been gone for so long. When we opened the door and saw them, they were sitting in front of the television on the floor; they turned around, looked at us and said "hi", and continued watching TV. My heart sank. I thought what had this woman done to my children? I knew from that day on, I would never leave my daughters like that again and definitely not leave them with her. It wasn't until many years later that my oldest daughter told me what my mother said to them. My mother told my daughters, "when your parents get here, I don't want you running and jumping all over the place, just sit there on the floor." I was so angry with her for doing that to my girls. She had been dead for a few years when I found this out. But my anger for her increased and there was no way to confront her with what she had done. I felt guilty for leaving my daughters, I felt horrible for subjecting my daughters to their grandmother's behavior. She was supposed to be a bright spot in their lives but she turned out to be a source of disappointment and anxiety. There are some challenges that my daughter's are working through as adults that may stem from the treatment they received from their grandmother. This tears me up inside. My daughters did not deserve to be treated like that. My girls were sweet, talented and loving and deserved to be treated in the same manner. My mother baby-sat for other people's children and she treated them better than she treated her own grandchildren or me.

When I found out a few years ago that my godmother tied me to a chair when I was a young child, I became angrier with my mother because she continued to allow this woman to be my godmother. She continued to expect me to respect this woman who traumatized me at such a young age. How can I forgive her?

Putting the Pieces Together

I have tried hard for years to forgive Ruth (not her real name), my adopted mother for how she treated me. But I realized one day that sometimes the way people treat us has nothing to do with us but someone else or something else. In my case it was my adopted mother and what I believe to be her deeply embedded anger for Joan, her sister, my biological mother. One day I was talking to my half sister about how my adopted mother treated me growing up. As we talked she said she might know the reason Ruth treated me the way she did. She asked me if I knew about her abortion? I looked at her in total shock and said "what abortion?" She told me when Ruth was a teenager she became pregnant and was scared to death to tell her mother so she begged my biological mother, Joan (not her real name) to help her abort her baby. Abortions at that time involved a coat hanger. Needless to say that was a horrifying experience for both of them. You may ask what this has to do with me since this occurred many years before I was born. Because of this dangerous abortion, Ruth developed problems years later and had to have a hysterectomy and could not have children. She wanted children more than anything. But Joan went on to have five children with her husband and became pregnant with me because of an extra marital affair. Ruth adopted me to save her sister from whatever stigma or problems she would face. A light came on in my head as my sister told me about this little known secret. Even though Ruth begged Joan to help with her abortion years ago, her adopting me was like Joan giving her, a baby back. But it is also possible Ruth held a grudge against Joan because she had so many babies and Ruth couldn't have any. Now Ruth has to raise Joan's illegitimate child. I believe Ruth took her anger for Joan out on me. I mentioned this to my therapist and she was impressed that I was able to put these points together and come to that conclusion. I tried for many years to look at things from Ruth's point of view but this one really made sense. This is how Ruth coped with her situation and anger towards her sister.

The Transition

Even after learning about Ruth's deep dark secret, I was still having trouble forgiving her for her treatment of me. After all it wasn't my fault Joan helped Ruth with her abortion; it wasn't my fault that I was the product of an affair. But! There is always a "But". But after I allowed myself to sit in my pain of anger, hurt and resentment, I asked myself, how does my anger affect her? It doesn't because she is no longer here. It's obvious she didn't care then. She really doesn't care now. This situation is all on me. I had to ask myself some hard questions. How do I clear this negative energy from my life? How does this negative energy block me from accomplishing the goals in my life? Does this negative energy of un-forgiveness prevent me from losing this excess weight I've been struggling with? Is this un-forgiveness responsible for the chronic pains in my body? Is this un-forgiveness responsible for my inability to have a good healthy relationship? Is it responsible for my bouts of depression?

According to my hero Louise Hay the answer is yes to all of these questions.

> *"You can never be free of bitterness as long as you continue to think unforgiving thoughts. How can you be happy in this moment if you continue to choose to be angry and resentful? Thoughts of bitterness can't create joy. No matter how justified you feel you are, no matter what "they" did, if you insist on holding on to the past, then you will never be free. Forgiving yourself and others will release you from the prison of the past."*
>
> http://www.louisehay.com/forgiveness/

As I write this book, it is obvious I am still struggling with forgiving my adopted mother and my godmother for their treatment of my daughters and me. But I do realize that for the sake of my soul, my sanity and my life, I must continue to strive for complete and total forgiveness. This has controlled my life long enough. Even though I cannot offer my healing story for this subject, know that I am on my journey of forgiving not only my adopted mother but also everyone who I feel has wronged me. Peeling back this layer could and will probably assist in the peeling back of other layers that I have been struggling to complete. Louise Hay helps me to understand that this un-forgiveness can and does cause other problems we face in our lives.

> *"When you don't flow freely with life in the present moment, it usually means that you're holding on to a past moment. It can be regret, sadness, hurt, fear, guilt, blame, anger, resentment, or sometimes even a desire for revenge. Each one of these states comes from a space of un-forgiveness, a refusal to let go and come in to the present moment. Only in the present moment can you create your future."*
>
> http://www.louisehay.com/forgiveness/

I include quotes from Louise Hay because she is the author who helped me begin this journey. Her story helps me realize that forgiveness can occur with pains so deep that even remembering that they occurred is difficult. I have even told others how important forgiveness is. If not achieved it can be like a cancer that can metastasize throughout our lives.

As I was browsing through Facebook one day, I saw this quote from an unknown author that makes it very plain.

> *"Not forgiving someone is like taking poison and expecting them to die."*
>
> *Author Unknown*

WOW. Just WOW. It can't be any simpler than that. But our mind tells us it isn't that simple. We can come up with many, many reasons to justify why we are not able to forgive the person who wronged us. But what we have to understand is, we are not condoning their behavior by forgiving them, but we are letting go of the baggage we are carrying around. Louise Hay speaks to this dilemma.

> "When you blame another, you give your own power away because you're placing the responsibility for your feelings on someone else. People in your life may behave in ways that trigger uncomfortable responses in you. However, they didn't get into your mind and create the buttons that have mastering your "ability to respond." In other words, you learn to consciously choose rather than simply react."
>
> http://www.louisehay.com/forgiveness/

Money Matters

Asking my mother for money was always mental torture. When my husband and me got in a bind and needed to ask her for a loan, she put me through the 3rd degree. She worried us until we paid her back. Even before that, she really didn't teach me to save, she would say it but when I got in a position to save while I was living at home after college, she made me pay her rent every month. And got mad when I was late. All the times my brother lived at home after high school, (he didn't even go to college) he never had to pay rent.

After I moved out on my own, which was an awkward transition because I got fed up with my mother trying to tell me how to run my life so I left out of anger. But whenever I made a bad decision I could hear my mother say in my head "your hamscammy". That word haunts me to this day.

My mother was very controlling and knew how to humiliate me and make me feel bad about myself. One day I told my mother I was pregnant with my second daughter. Instead of her being happy for us she said, "I don't know why you want another one, you can't take care of the one you have". My happiness was blocked by her sharp uncaring words. She felt she had all the answers and everyone else was wrong. These things along with her inability to show love and acceptance towards me caused my self-esteem to suffer greatly. I promised myself that when I grew up I would do the opposite of what she did because I didn't want to be anything like her. Unfortunately that way of thinking has caused me financial problems. She paid all her bills on time and had a high credit score and was able to get loans and all types of credit. I had done just the opposite. I refuse to get any credit cards and struggle to pay all my bills on time. I haven't been good at saving money and my credit score has been low more than it has been high. I have not consciously been a slow bill payer but sub-consciously I believe this is what has happened. There is always a reason why but I spend many hours wondering why my financial life is in such shambles. When I put forth a gallant effort, things still come crashing down. Then one day I had to think back on the promise I made myself. Be the opposite of my mother. I then realize that I have to make better promises to myself. I cannot live my life being like her or being the opposite of her, I have to be the best me I can be. I heard this in one of the affirmation recordings I listen to that is helping me along this journey. It says;

> *I now allow myself to let go of the need to hold on to thoughts and beliefs about success and abundance that have been blocking my growth. Most of these thoughts and beliefs are not even mine. I have unconsciously been programed by society and other people on my journey here on earth. But here I am. This is a new day. I am now choosing to consciously reprogram myself for the higher good. I allow myself to let go of old energy that is not even mine. I have been holding on to it for too long. I am accepting my past. Because acceptance opens up the door of change. If I do not accept it I cannot change. Acceptance is the key to freedom. I have that key. It is safe to let go now.*

I AM AFFIRMATIONS: SPIRITUAL ABUNDANCE, PROSPERITY & SUCCESS

As this layer of forgiveness inches its way back, my financial life will improve as well because I will no longer hold myself to promises that are self-defeating. Once I realized that my decisions have no effect on her, I had to begin to seriously dig deeper into the rest of the emotional blocks that were holding me back.

In the book "The Emotion Code", Dr. Bradley Nelson talks about "trapped emotions". He says,

> *"Trapped emotions are truly epidemic, and are the insidious, invisible cause of much suffering and illness, both physical and emotional in nature."*
> The Emotion Code – Dr. Bradley Nelson, pg. 21

Specifically to the point of how we treat each other he says,
> *"So much of human suffering is because we don't know what we do to one another. If only we could understand that what we do to others, we do to ourselves."*
> The Emotion Code – Dr. Bradley Nelson, pg 350

The greatest lesson and example of forgiveness is known worldwide and for thousands of generations, *"Father forgive them, for they know not what they do."* If Christians, just Christians would practice this one lesson taught by Jesus, this entire world would be a better place.

I have highlighted a few ways in which we can peel back that layer of forgiveness. But it is going to take a lot of effort and determination on our part. Prayer can help but each person has to do his or her own internal work. Just as I had to sit in my pain and allow it to flow this can help to peel back this hurtful layer. As long as it doesn't drive us to act out our hurt on anyone especially the one who hurt us. This is our pain, our "trapped emotions" that we have to deal with. There is already too much violence in our society. People are killing and hurting each other over stupid stuff. We have to learn how to let that stuff go. It really does not add love, joy or peace to our lives when we act out like this.

Save yourself and forgive someone today.

Chapter 11

Secrets & Lies

POEM

"What you don't know can't hurt you," so we've been told
    What lies society teaches us
    Lying and keeping the secrets that surround me
        kept me from finding out what laid my foundation
    That hurts
They lied to protect themselves
    They lied to keep their secrets a secret
        They acted like it was for my best but it was really
As I find out the secrets
        that so many other people knew
I realized it was not a secret to anyone - but me
Once I discovered the truth, I fit the pieces together and things begin to make sense.

Avoidance

It was in my plans to not include this chapter in my book. But when I thought about it, the other layers probably would not exist for me if it were not for the "secrets and lies" that surround my life. This was yet another attempt to avoid dealing with this layer. I cannot avoid it. I must deal with it if I am going to peel it away and heal from the scars it has left.

The Family Secret

Many families have secrets. The secret affair, the secret illness, the secret fortune and the secret child, are some of the skeletons families keep locked away, hidden from the outside world and un-approachable in conversations within the family. But we don't realize that even though these secrets are not discussed, they continue to rule over certain people in the family. Even though that secret is tucked away in the back of the minds of the family members who are privileged, or cursed with the sorted details, it has control over them. During the time the secret originated, lies were told, information was hidden and everyone involved had to be careful what they said and whom they said it to. They also have to remember the lies they told in case they had to re-tell it or add something to it.

In my case, I was the family secret. I was the secret child, the result of a love affair my mother had with her friends husband. My mother was married but her husband was in jail and she had 5 other children. To keep me a secret she first tried to abort me as I mentioned earlier. So her sister told her she would adopt her baby and raise it as her own. OK problem solved.

Sensing Something

Throughout my childhood, there were things said that made me wonder. My cousin said one day during an argument, "you're our sister anyway". I didn't know what she meant at the time, but as an adult, I remember those important moments and comments. During my early 20's my biological mother's ex-husband (who I had never met before) said to me while we were attending a family funeral, "so you're the adopted one". By that time, I knew I was adopted and who my real mother was, but if I hadn't known, that statement would have crushed my world.

Holding onto The Secret

People can use a family secret as leverage over other family members. That secret can also destroy lives as that information can eat away at someone's insides like a cancer, wondering if they should tell or if they should keep holding onto that secret. Many times that secret can come out at very uncomfortable times creating anger and resentment for those involved. This information when told by the wrong person and in the wrong way, can and has crushed a person's whole sense of identity.

Because my aunt adopted me, they felt their secret was safe. They were the only two who knew who my biological father was. Even he didn't know. Immediately after I was born on my mother's dining room table, I was taken in a clothesbasket to my aunt's house. She was married to a minister and they had a 4-year-old adopted son. Abandonment and rejection has already occurred in my life with the talk of abortion and discussion of what would happen to me. All of this occurred before I was born.

The Effects of Being The Secret

I didn't' really feel the effects of being the family secret until I got older. I could feel that something was going on as a child but I didn't know what it was. I just felt out of place. When I turned 17 years old, my adopted mother told me that I was adopted and that the woman I had been calling my aunt was really my biological mother. She said at the time that she didn't know my biological father's name but he was light skinned with wavy hair and that I looked like him.

The Secret Partially Revealed

Everything changed one day when I was 22 years old. My biological mother was having a conversation with a man at church and introduced me to him. We said hello and I kept going. It wasn't until the next day that she told me that he was my biological father. I was in a state of shock. I hadn't paid that much attention to him so I couldn't remember what he looked like. She told me his name and told me that his wife was one of her friends at the time I was born so she never told him about me. Needless to say I wanted to meet him.

Helping to Keep The Secret

Donald, the man I was dating at the time who would eventually be my husband helped me get a letter to my father with the story I was told and pictures of myself. Donald was very instrumental in helping me connect with my father because he knew how painful those secrets could be. He too was part of a secret. His ex-wife refused to tell their daughter that he was her father. Their marriage ended when their daughter was a baby. Soon afterwards, his ex-wife married another man and Donald's daughter grew up never knowing who her biological father was. I saw his pain from the opposite side of the situation. This pain is real.

After receiving my letter, my father called me and we met as father and daughter for the first time. We began a father/daughter relationship, seeing each other when we could. He felt he could not tell his wife about me for fear she would leave him. So he kept me a secret. I had to sneak and see my father without telling anyone except my boyfriend. I knew my biological mother would be upset because she didn't want her secret out. My adopted mother would also be upset as well just because. Now I was keeping the family secret of myself, to myself. I wanted to tell it to everyone but I would hurt my father, my mother and others in the family who have held this secret. This is when it is a curse to be a caring person. I cared more about everyone else's feelings but dismissed mine. I wanted to spend more time with my father but he could only see me during errands so his wife would not find out where he was going or whom he was meeting. Needless to say, I felt like a mistress instead of his daughter.

More Family

After a few months my father did let his brother and sister know about me. They also lived in Detroit. I also got the chance to meet my grandmother who came to visit one summer. I had a whole family that I didn't know. I felt so cheated. When I was alone, I got angry about it. I have 8 aunts and uncles that I have never known. I have had a grandmother all this time and I never knew it. I have many, many cousins who I have never met all because I was kept a secret. And I still couldn't spend time with them because my father's wife may find out. My dad would get on edge at times when he talked about it to me. I knew he had a bad heart so I didn't want to do anything that would upset him. But I was suffering. I didn't know how to deal with that pain.

Knowing that I was a secret caused me to feel like I was unimportant. I felt invisible so many times. I felt like I was not important enough for everyone to know who I was, who I really was.

Feeling the Connection

One year I had this uncontrollable urge to travel to Arkansas to visit my grandmother. My husband told me if it was that strong that I needed to go. I flew down and while I was there I visited my other aunts for the first time. I had 3 aunts and more cousins that I got to meet. My dad had finally told them about me. Everyone was so welcoming and accepting. I spend the next day at the hospital visiting my grandmother. The next weekend she passed away. Even though I had only seen my grandmother 1 time before that, we still had a connection so strong that I knew I needed to see her before she died. As a woman in my thirties, I can't help but think about all the time I could have spent with my grandmother, gaining her wisdom, being held in her arms and knowing that I belonged.

Even though I was spending time with my newfound relatives, I still felt like the secrecy was continuing. My father could tell everyone in his family about me except his wife. I told him I understood and would not pressure him to do what he felt he couldn't do but I didn't understand what I was doing to myself until years later. Telling his family made them part of the secret conspiracy. Now they had to make sure that my dad's wife didn't find out.

Secret Regrets

One day I got word that my father was very ill. I left in the middle of a class I was taking and rushed to the hospital to see my father. He looked very ill and in a lot of pain. He was glad to see me but then became very uncomfortable that I was there because he didn't know when his wife would show up. He didn't want her to see me. His doctor came in and he got a bit agitated so I said goodbye and I left. Out of all the years I had been a secret, that moment hurt the worst. I couldn't be there for my father to help him through his illness. I couldn't bring comfort to my father, only distress. I couldn't show my love for my father during a time when he really needed me. This created a pain within me so great that I thought I was going to lose it. A few weeks later, I got the call that my father had passed away. I went to talk to my cousin Albert, who was my closest relative on my father's side. He always made me feel accepted. He told me some things that my dad said to him about me. How he regretted not telling his wife about me. How he really loved me and was sorry that he couldn't be a better father to me. I felt good to hear this but I was still hurting on the inside.

Feeling Left Out

When people read my father's obituary, there is no mention of me. I wanted to get up during the funeral and scream, "he's my father". But I didn't, I kept it inside but it felt like a bomb was going to explode within. How do I grieve, how do I find comfort within myself that my father is gone? I wanted to comfort his wife, but I couldn't. I looked at her and I felt bad that I was part of many lies that my father told just to see me.

For years afterwards, I was angry. Angry with everyone who lied and worked so damn hard to keep me a secret. Was I not good enough for others to know about? What was wrong with me that I had to be kept a secret?

Tired of Being a Secret

After my dad had been dead for about 3 years, I decided to tell his wife who I was. I had been thinking about it since he passed away but I finally felt the time was right. I called her and told her I was a member of the family and wanted to come by and see her. She invited me to her home. I was very nervous but was determined to have this conversation. I told her everything. To my surprise, she wasn't angry but very understanding. She allowed me to visit her often. She even invited my daughters over and she cooked for us. She told me she wished my father had told her about me. We could have spent a lot of time together. I finally stopped feeling like a secret but accepted for who I was.

There are some people who may still feel that I should not have expose this secret. Many already know but some feel that the secret should still be hidden. My question to them is, at what point do my feelings matter? At what point do I get to break free from the cloud of secrecy and lies? Aren't my feelings important? Don't I matter just as much as anyone else who might be hurt by the truth? These are actually questions that I had to answer for myself. I had to feel like my feelings mattered. I had to feel like my feelings were important. I had to allow myself to break free from the cloud of secrecy and lies. During the twenty-five years that I was able to have a limited father/daughter relationship with my father, these very questions were constantly flowing though my mind. Even after I told a close friend that I told my father's wife about me, he asked, "Why would you do that?" My answer to him was, "because I am tired to being a secret". That is my response to everyone who questions my actions of telling the truth, "I AM TIRED OF BEING A SECRET". No one knows that pain that comes with being the family secret, living a lie, not being able to live into the person that I truly am meant to me because of the limitations of being "the family secret".

Other Layers Created by Being The Secret

The layers of low self-esteem, acceptance, abandonment and rejection, denial, anger, regret, fear, trust and forgiveness for me all stem from my life starting off as the family secret.

It has taken me years of work to get to this point of allowing this to flow from me. Some of the pain subsided as I started a relationship with my father's wife. I made several visits to her house, sat in my daddy chair and ate at the table where he ate. But after she developed severe symptoms of dementia, I was no longer able to visit her. Her mind told her I was my father's mistress instead of his daughter. This added a whole new dimension to my challenges. Remember I said I felt like his mistress when we met because we had to meet in secrecy. Those feelings returned and that connection I had with my dad's wife was gone.

The Work

In recognition and acceptance of who I am, I have been on the road to healing. I understood early on that this is a journey and not a destination. I had to get use to the idea that some people will not accept my truth. After talking to my aunt, my father's sister in law, she told me that one of my father's sisters did not believe that I was his daughter. She felt that I was lying about it. That caused me to pull back from getting too close to any of my relatives on my father's side because I felt I couldn't deal with any more rejection. I had 2 cousins reach out to me when I lived in the Chicago land area. We talked on the phone and really got to know each other. But that fear of rejection inside me would not allow me to get any closer. I apologize to my cousins, aunts and uncles who I was not able to get closer to because of my fear of being rejected and not accepted as Albert Bone's daughter. Feeling that I wasn't worthy enough for my father to tell his wife about me was very difficult for me to live with. Even after shouldering that burden for so long, the idea of being rejected by anyone else in the family has been something that I have just not been able to gain enough strength for yet.

As you can see I have a lot to do in this area of my life. It's all internal work that has to be done. Peeling back this layer can and will help me peel back the other layers that I have struggled with during my life.

Feeling Worthy

I said in two paragraphs back "I wasn't worthy enough for my father to tell his wife about me". Some may think that me being worthy may not have been the case for my father. But I use the word worthy because this is what living as a secret takes away. The feeling of being worthy has been something I have not felt until I made it my aim to heal from this. Making an effort to feel worthy even when I was not treated like I was worthy, feeling like I am accepted when I was not treated like I was accepted, feeling that I matter even though I was not treated like I mattered all play a part in my healing. I have to feel worthy and accepted so that I matter to myself no matter what is going on around me or to me.

New Habits

I have to form new habits in order to make long lasting change in my life. Those negative feelings and thoughts of being a secret somewhat paralyzed me for a long time. They paralyzed my mind by thinking that I wasn't good enough and paralyzed my heart in feeling that I wasn't worthy of love. My new habits involved loving myself no matter what other people say or do and knowing that I am worthy of love, joy and happiness in my life.

Chapter 12

Conclusion

POEM

My light has not been seen for a while. The qualities of my inner self are hidden from view. Darkness has been a habit for so long, would I know the light if I saw it?

I search for the switch that will illuminate the best parts of me. I search through the muck and mire of doubt, rejection and fear only to become comfortable in this dark existence.

But my guides are helping me one after another to find my way to my light. Each one takes me so far and then hands me to another showing me the way. As I travel through this darkness I now have a clearer purpose, a new determination to find my light switch.

I no longer feel comfortable in the stagnation of the layers that cover my soul. My smile and laughter are no longer a forced attempt at my authentic self.
I love me, I really, really love me.
I feel genuine joy and acceptance for myself.
I have found the switch and my light is now shining brightly for the world to see.

Decide to Heal

It's easy to get stuck in a pity party licking our wounds and dwelling on all the people and things that have worked against us. All of the layers we have looked at and even others that I have not touched on can weigh us down. But they can also become a familiar friend and the thought of change and venturing out into the unknown can scare the crap out of us. Even if the results are healing, prosperity, abundance and love, we are not familiar with this unknown reality and may not feel worthy of having them.

Many times as we attempt to deal with our various layers we cover them up with addictions. These layers are breading grounds for producing alcoholics, drug addicts, sex addicts, food addicts, etc. Some people may also revert to seemingly positive means to hide or ignore their pain. This can take the form of workaholics, helicopter parenting, overexertion, excessive shopping, and excessive exercising. All of these can be considered escapism from the underlying problem.

I realize this seems like a lot of layers and the thought of dealing with so many can be overwhelming. But as I pointed out before, many of the layers can actually link together as one can cause a chain reaction and be responsible for others. But there is one way of looking at this in a positive sense. When the initial layer is realized and the process of peeling it away has occurred, the layers that are linked to it may peel away simultaneously.

In order to heal, I feel we have to journey back to the time and place that the hurt occurred. We have to face it, confront it. The best way to conquer fear and past hurts is to admit it and sit in the pain that it causes. Allow those feelings to flow because they are your feelings and they must be recognized. We have spent too much time ignoring them and running from them and because of these actions, they keep control of our lives. It rears its ugly head in ways that we don't expect. Take back control and fact it head on. Then the healing can begin. This is something my adopted mother Ruth never did. I knew something was eating away at her so one day I decided to ask her point blank what happened in her life that caused her so much pain. She lost it. She started shaking her head in a fit of rage and said, "I can't talk about it. Just leave me alone." This scared the crap out of me and I never asked again. Because she would not talk about her deep dark secret, she became a very angry old person. Her conversation was always negative with just about everything. The older generation thought that if they didn't talk about the painful events in their lives they would just go away. But they don't go away. As I said before that pain grows and festers like a cancer. It eats away at us and can take away any joy we could have had. I did not want that to happen to me. That's way I needed to write this book.

Healing Takes Time

During my times of aloneness, I continue to inch my way along my journey of healing. Many times I don't feel like any of what I was doing is helping me. I read inspirational books, listened to people like Louise Hay talk about her techniques of becoming free from the bondage of mental, physical and emotional prisons of abuse. I listened to Dr. Wayne Dyer talk about how there is a spiritual solution to every problem. I read books and articles on clearing my chakras, the energy zones in the body. Of course I read the Bible and listened to sermons and even meditated but nothing was helping me reach the goals I was hoping they would. I did have spurts of genuine joy and peace but it was short lived. I became frustrated and the majority of the time I was surviving in a state of mere existence rather than living my life to the fullest. At times I felt that this journey was long and difficult to travel. Then I would get a glimmer of reality that helped me put things in better perspective. I remembered that my journey to this point has taken 56 years. That pain began when I was a small child, influenced by the trusted adults around me in a society where children were to be seen and not heard, in a culture that kept deep dark secrets and never talked about them nor allow children to ask questions about them. As an introvert I kept my questions to myself even when I became an adult. I was bound by the "respect my elders" code and felt if my parents, adopted and biological, wanted to answer my un-questioned questions, they would. I've been carrying those unanswered questions and that pain they produced, with me for 56 years. Certainly it would take me longer than a few months or even a year to overcome them. I also realized that once I started on this journey of healing that there was no turning back. For me turning back meant to return to the old way of denial that did not lead to healing. I have to stay on the road to healing. Because one thing I realized is that in order to find peace, joy and love, I must remain on my journey toward healing. I don't have to wait until I get to the end of this journey, which may take years, I can experience true joy, peace and love along the way. This is so much better that reverting back to living a false life of denial, sadness and defeat. I've been stuck there long enough.

We are all Connected

As I continue on this journey, I am lead to more practices and understandings that connect me in a whole new way to my Creator, My God, The Divine. I am realizing that even though I am an individual I am also connected to all of creation. I love being out in nature and gazing up at the stars. We are all connected to everything and everyone. We are more than the physical reality that we are so focused on everyday. We are more than our mind. We are more than our past. We are more than our hurts, disappointments and rejections. Everything I've been reading and listening to focus on the main point that we are all spiritual beings existing in a physical body. But most of us rely on and put too much stake into the physical side of ourselves and put barriers up to block out our spiritual side. Those barriers are the layers covering our soul. Our soul, the core of our soul after the layers have been pulled back connects with our spirit, that part of us that is able to transmit the information that we need to live into our authentic selves, the real us.

Don't you want to know who you were truly meant to be? Don't you want to know who you are and why you are here? Peeling back those layers that I covered in this book and many others that I have not mentioned can reveal the answers to those questions.

It has been about five years since I have been focusing on my journey toward total healing. Five years is a short time compared to 56 years but at times it seems just as long. But I can honesty say that my time has been well spent as I have gained more knowledge about who I am and some of my questions have been answered. I have also learned how to be OK with the questions that will never be answered.

Uniqueness

Our soul is as unique as our personality. The ego wants us to be like others or wants others to be like us. So some of us strive to be a part of the group while others strive to have the group be like them. Our soul is hidden behind the layers of the ego and fights to be it's unique self. So there is a tug of war going on when the soul is calling we feel it but we push it down because it is out of our comfort zone of the ego's control. The ego fights to fit in. Abraham Hicks calls it "being out of vibrational alignment" from our higher self, the universe, our creator, God.

Desire to be Healed

The questions is – "Do we want to be healed? Healed from depression, hurt, emotional abuse, physical abuse, verbal abuse, low self-esteem, lack, fear, doubt, etc.? The reason I pose this question is that sometimes we get so use to the negative things in our lives they become normal, comfortable and a way of life for us. It can be our comfort zone because we know it so well. But just like Jesus asked the man who had been ill for 38 years and was lying by the healing pool of Bethesda, "Do you want to be healed? It was a confusing question because one would assume that if the man were lying by a pool that was known for it's healing; his desire would be to be healed. But instead of answering Jesus by saying, "yes, I want to be healed", his response was filled with excuses as to why he had not been healed in the pool. Jesus had to wake the man up from the sleep of sameness and make him aware of the actual reality of healing. What we have to ask ourselves honestly is, are we willing to step into the unknown reality of being healed? Are we ready to step out of the box of our comfort zone of despair, fear and doubt and wrap our mind around happiness, joy, love and acceptance?

Answering the Question

At the beginning of this book I posed another question "What's wrong with me? I'm going full circle, back to the beginning questions in this book. As I have started to peel back the layers that have overshadowed my soul, my question changed from "What's Wrong With Me? To "Who Am I? This is the proper question to ask because from this question a whole new world of knowledge and discovery can open up. Asking the question "Who Am I?, forced me to look not at my physical existence but my entire existence. Seeing myself from a different perspective allows me to wonder, who am I apart from what I do, apart from where I am, apart from what I look like? This journey of discovery leads us to wonder why God created us and planted us in our family, at this time, and in this situation? But how do we get to the point where there is a shift from asking "What's Wrong With Me? To "Who Am I"? That's what I have attempted to do in this book. I have highlighted various layers that can encompass our lives that prevent us from being our true authentic selves. They are roadblocks that stunt our growth and can and do keep us locked into a proverbial box of self-imposed limitations. The layers or chapters I have chosen may not represent all the layers that each person reading this book may be dealing with. Some layers may be absent from this book that some people may have experienced, but this book is only a beginning as to how to recognize the layers and how to work on peeling them back in order to uncover the authentic soul.

All of what we perceive as obstacles to discovering and being conscious of our soul is really a journey to self-discovery. We know what is right for us. We just have to dig deep inside of ourselves to find it. We have been blinded and held captive by the thoughts and actions of other people's interpretation of who we are and what our truth is. Our truth is buried deep within our soul. As we peel back the layers we will reveal the lies that other people have told about ourselves. We can then free ourselves from the shackles of misinterpretation of the truth. Healing will begin when we grow weary of the misinterpretations of the truth about God and about ourselves.

Blessings to you as you embark on your journey towards healing. Be kind to yourself and don't get discourage if it doesn't progress as fast as you would like it to. Enjoy the journey. Most of all forgive yourself and love yourself. You are worthy.

Resources

DR. WAYNE DYER'S
"10 Secrets for Success and Inner Peace"
http://www.drwaynedyer.com/blog/move-back-to-love/

Bishop Timothy Clark
"Recycled Evil"
https://www.youtube.com/watch?v=NuncFouJak8

Louise Hay
1. https://play.google.com/store/apps/details?id=com.louise.daily
2. http://www.louisehay.com/3-habits-building-self-esteem/
3. *You Can Heal Your Life*, Published January 1, 1984 by Hay House. Kindle Edition.
4. http://www.louisehay.com/forgiveness/

Eckhart Tolle
The Power of Now, Published August 19th 2004 by Namaste Publishing

151 Affirmations
http://151affirmations.com/free-affirmations-ebook-download/

Just Organic Medicine
http://justorganicmedicine.com/psychologists-warn-never-use-these-5-phrases-when-talking-to-your-child/

Dr. Bradley Nelson
"The Emotion Code", Published June 2007 by Wellness Unmasked Publishing

PowerThoughts Meditation Club
I Am Affirmations: Spiritual Abundance, Prosperity & Success
HTTPS://WWW.YOUTUBE.COM/WATCH?V=XEM-A0AHLU0&T=563S

About the Author

A. Annette Hankins is a native Detroiter and holds a BA from Wayne State University and a Master of Divinity from Garrett-Evangelical Theological Seminary in Evanston, Illinois. She is an Ordained Baptist Minister. She also worked in the television and media business for over 30 years is various crew positions but truly excelled as a sound technician and Emmy Awarding Video Editor. Annette speaks not as a professional in Onion of the Soul but as someone who has lived what she speaks about. Her desire is to help others who have or are living with these layers and point them in the direction of healing. She also desires to help those who are perpetrators who cause negative situations in other people's lives. There is enough healing to go around for everyone. Annette has 2 wonderful grown daughters, a wonderful son-in-law and 2 beautiful and intelligent twin granddaughters.

Other Courses

Mind — Meditation ← Melli + SOS
  Headspace
  mindfulness.com
  Headstrong
  Mental Strength School

432 Hz miracle music

Body — Sensate — nervous system
  Ex
  H.E / Vits / herbs / water

Donna Eden Energy course
Mindvalley.com

→ Let my triggers be my teacher. Saved under Keep on my phone.

→ Write up soul / lonely list in my diary &
→ other courses

"I am safe, It is safe to feel. My feelings are normal & acceptable"

ex I am capable & I can do this. I want to be healthier for myself.